Gil G. Noam
Editor-in-Chief

NEW DIRECTIONS FOR YOUTH DEVELOPMENT

Theory
Practice
Research

spring | 2006

Youth Leadership

Foreword by Ronald Heifetz

Max Klau
Steve Boyd
Lynn Luckow

issue editors

JOSSEY-BASS™
An Imprint of
WILEY

YOUTH LEADERSHIP
Max Klau, Steve Boyd, Lynn Luckow (eds.)
New Directions for Youth Development, No. 109, Spring 2006
Gil G. Noam, Editor-in-Chief

Copyright © 2006 Wiley Periodicals, Inc., A Wiley Company. All rights reserved. No part of this publication may be reproduced in any form or by any means, except as permitted under sections 107 and 108 of the 1976 United States Copyright Act, without either the prior written permission of the publisher or authorization through the Copyright Clearance Center, 222 Rosewood Drive, Danvers, MA 01923; (978) 750-8400; fax (978) 646-8600. The copyright notice appearing at the bottom of the first page of an article in this journal indicates the copyright holder's consent that copies may be made for personal or internal use, or for personal or internal use of specific clients, on the condition that the copier pay for copying beyond that permitted by law. This consent does not extend to other kinds of copying, such as copying for general distribution, for advertising or promotional purposes, for creating collective works, or for resale. Such permission requests and other permission inquiries should be addressed to the Permissions Department, c/o John Wiley & Sons, Inc., 111 River Street, Hoboken, NJ 07030; (201) 748-6011, fax (201) 748-6008, www.wiley.com/go/permissions.

Microfilm copies of issues and articles are available in 16mm and 35mm, as well as microfiche in 105mm, through University Microfilms Inc., 300 North Zeeb Road, Ann Arbor, Michigan 48106-1346.

NEW DIRECTIONS FOR YOUTH DEVELOPMENT (ISSN 1533-8916, electronic ISSN 1537-5781) is part of The Jossey-Bass Psychology Series and is published quarterly by Wiley Subscription Services, Inc., A Wiley Company, at Jossey-Bass, 989 Market Street, San Francisco, California 94103-1741. POSTMASTER: Send address changes to New Directions for Youth Development, Jossey-Bass, 989 Market Street, San Francisco, California 94103-1741.

SUBSCRIPTIONS cost $80.00 for individuals and $180.00 for institutions, agencies, and libraries. Prices subject to change. Refer to the order form at the back of this issue.

EDITORIAL CORRESPONDENCE should be sent to the Editor-in-Chief, Dr. Gil G. Noam, McLean Hospital, 115 Mill Street, Belmont, MA 02478.

Cover photograph by Age Fotostock

www.josseybass.com

Gil G. Noam, Editor-in-Chief
Harvard University and McLean Hospital

Editorial Board

K. Anthony Appiah
Princeton University
Princeton, N.J.

Peter Benson
Search Institute
Minneapolis, Minn.

Dale Blythe
University of Minnesota
Minneapolis, Minn.

Dante Cicchetti
University of Rochester
Rochester, N.Y.

William Damon
Stanford University
Palo Alto, Calif.

Goéry Delacôte
The Exploratorium
San Francisco, Calif.

Felton Earls
Harvard Medical School
Boston, Mass.

Jacquelynne S. Eccles
University of Michigan
Ann Arbor, Mich.

Wolfgang Edelstein
Max Planck Institute for Human Development
Berlin, Germany

Kurt Fischer
Harvard Graduate School of Education
Cambridge, Mass.

Carol Gilligan
New York University Law School
New York, N.Y.

Robert Granger
W. T. Grant Foundation
New York, N.Y.

Reed Larson
University of Illinois at Urbana-Champaign
Urbana-Champaign, Ill.

Richard Lerner
Tufts University
Medford, Mass.

Milbrey W. McLaughlin
Stanford University
Stanford, Calif.

Pedro Noguera
New York University
New York, N.Y.

Fritz Oser
University of Fribourg
Fribourg, Switzerland

Karen Pittman
The Forum for Youth Investment
Washington, D.C.

Jane Quinn
The Children's Aid Society
New York, N.Y.

Jean Rhodes
University of Massachusetts, Boston
Boston, Mass.

Rainer Silbereisen
University of Jena
Jena, Germany

Elizabeth Stage
University of California at Berkeley
Berkeley, Calif.

Hans Steiner
Stanford Medical School
Stanford, Calif.

Carola Suárez-Orozco
New York University
New York, N.Y.

Marcelo Suárez-Orozco
New York University
New York, N.Y.

Erin Cooney, Editorial Assistant
McLean Hospital

Contents

Foreword *1*
  Ronald Heifetz

Editors' Notes *3*
  Max Klau, Steve Boyd, Lynn Luckow

Executive Summary *9*

1. The mystery of youth leadership development: The path to just communities *13*
   Margaret Libby, Maureen Sedonaen, Steven Bliss
   The authors seek to bring clarity to the discourse on youth leadership and introduce the concept of "inside" versus "outside" leadership as a valuable framework for understanding the term.

2. Bridging generations: Applying "adult" leadership theories to youth leadership development *27*
   Carole A. MacNeil
   There is a wealth of literature devoted to adult leadership, and very little exploring youth leadership. In this article, the author examines the connection between the two topics.

3. Youth leadership and youth development: Connections and questions *45*
   Cathann A. Kress
   The youth development movement is broadly interested in promoting strength and resilience as opposed to preventing problems and delinquency. The author argues that leadership represents one possible developmental pathway for youth and explores the implications of this perspective.

4. Exploring youth leadership in theory and practice: An empirical study *57*
   Max Klau
   In an effort to move from theory to practice, the author presents case studies based on direct observation of three youth leadership programs.

Special Section on youth leadership in action: Key programs and practices

5. Leading, learning, and unleashing potential: Youth leadership and civic engagement   *89*
   Wendy Wheeler with Carolyn Edlebeck

   The authors describe the Innovation Center's programs focusing on civic engagement as a tool for youth leadership development.

6. Moving from "youth leadership development" to "youth in governance": Learning leadership by doing leadership   *99*
   Carole A. MacNeil with Jennifer McClean

   The authors present the philosophy and experience behind the youth-adult partnerships fostered by 4-H's youth-in-governance programs.

7. Anytown: NCCJ's youth leadership experience in social justice   *107*
   Julia Matsudaira with Ashley Jefferson

   The authors describe an NCCJ youth leadership program focused on diversity and social justice.

8. Arts-based leadership: Theatrical tributes   *117*
   Eve Nussbaum Soumerai with Rachel Mazer

   The authors present a program that promotes youth leadership by involving young people in the creation and performance of theatrical tributes to well-known leaders of the past and present.

Resource Guide   *125*

Index   *129*

Foreword

IN RECENT DECADES, there has been a burgeoning interest in the theory and practice of leadership. Dozens of books exploring the practice of leadership in business, government, and the nonprofit world are published each year. We now have a professional organization (the International Leadership Association), a leading journal (*Leadership Quarterly*), and a growing number of academic programs devoted to the study and teaching of leadership.

In this context, it is only appropriate that scholars and practitioners begin to apply some disciplined attention to the challenges of youth leadership. As you will see in the pages that follow, there is a crowded landscape of programs that claim to teach youth leadership and surprisingly little scholarship devoted to understanding the work done by these programs.

With this issue of *New Directions for Youth Development*, editors Max Klau, Steve Boyd, and Lynn Luckow take an important step toward rectifying this imbalance. They have gathered together some of the most experienced and respected voices in the field to bring clarity and insight to basic and important questions. What is youth leadership? How is it different from adult leadership? How does it relate to the broader youth leadership movement? And exactly how is it taught by practitioners in the field today? In the pages ahead, you can expect to encounter thoughtful and informed engagement with these key questions.

My colleagues and I have argued that distinguishing leadership from authority opens up whole new possibilities for both leadership analysis and development. As we know intuitively, many people in high positions of authority do not exercise much leadership, and many people exercise significant leadership without much authority. The value of this distinction becomes readily apparent in the context of youth leadership. Young people are valuable stakeholders in their communities. They may not hold positions of authority, but they possess the potential to exercise leadership in meaningful ways. The contributors to this issue illuminate these opportunities and some of the developmental tasks that educators must concern themselves with to prepare youth for the challenges of leadership, not only when they "grow up" and take on authority positions but right now, when their generativity can itself contribute so much to innovation and renewal.

Today's young people are coming of age in a world facing a multitude of challenges. For educators, scholars, policymakers, and concerned adults, the question could hardly be clearer: How do we prepare them to be committed, empowered, effective, and engaged citizens both willing and able to make a positive difference in their communities? It is an important question deserving of a thoughtful and informed response.

With this issue, a collection of experienced scholars and practitioners share their insights on these questions. As you read these articles, do not expect simplistic assertions or easy answers. Rather, expect to be introduced to a lively, enthusiastic, and informed conversation among a group of passionate and knowledgeable experts. Together, they crystallize challenges, highlight debates, and share hard-earned wisdom.

Ronald Heifetz

RONALD HEIFETZ *is King Hussein bin Talal Lecturer in Public Leadership at Harvard's Kennedy School of Government, and cofounder of the Center for Public Leadership. He is a globally recognized expert on adult leadership, and author of two well-known books on the topic:* Leadership Without Easy Answers, *and* Leadership on the Line.

Editors' Notes

As academics, practitioners, and policymakers increasingly support models of positive psychology and youth development, the topic of youth leadership represents an intriguing frontier of inquiry. The notion of leadership moves beyond mere resilience; it implies an exceptional level of competence and mastery over oneself and an ability to influence others.

Despite the relevance of youth leadership to the field of youth development, however, the topic remains largely unexplored. The minimal amount of scholarly literature related to the topic barely scratches the surface and does not provide definitive answers to questions such as, *What exactly is youth leadership? Is it different from adult leadership? How does it differ from productive youth development? Can it be taught? If so, what are best and worst practices?*

The lack of scholarly attention is even more remarkable in light of the extensive educational infrastructure currently dedicated to youth leadership education. Across the nation, hundreds—perhaps thousands—of programs claim to teach young people leadership. Exactly what are these programs teaching? What do they do well? What do they do poorly? An informed understanding of youth leadership could support the work being done in programs that affect the lives of many thousands of young people every day.

The chapters collected in this volume shed light on emerging frontiers in theory, research, and practice related to youth leadership. We hope this issue of *New Directions for Youth Development* will help to bring some much needed insight, clarity, and attention to this important topic.

This volume is divided into two distinct sections. The first section presents an overview of youth leadership theory and research. In this section, we review existing literature, explore pertinent debates related to the topic, and present recent empirical research.

The second section focuses on youth leadership in action. In this section, we bring in voices from numerous practitioners—as well as the young people they work with—to understand better how youth leadership education actually happens in the field. What assumptions inform youth leadership education? How do these ideas inform practice? What are the results of participation in these programs and experiences?

With this edition of *New Directions for Youth Development*, we have sought to bring together scholars and practitioners with decades of involvement in youth leadership education. Our intention in gathering together this collection of writings has been to bring a new level of focus, rigor, and insight to this important discussion. While these articles provide no simple answers, they do crystallize a collection of seven issues and debates that are central to the discourse on youth leadership. In the pages ahead, expect to encounter the following core themes.

1. *The centrality of social justice to the discourse on youth leadership.* All of our contributors highlight a clear connection between the work of youth leadership and matters of social justice. In both theory and practice, they argue, youth leadership involves working toward a more inclusive, equal, and just society.

2. *Inside versus outside leadership.* In their article "The Mystery of Youth Leadership," authors Margaret Libby, Maureen Sedonaen, and Steven Bliss argue for the importance of distinguishing between "inside" and "outside" leadership. "Inside" leadership occurs inside existing formal institutions (such as schools, the Girl Scouts, community organizations, and so on) and involves the young people who have access and acceptance within those institutions. "Outside" leadership occurs outside of those institutions and involves young people who lack access and acceptance within those organizations. Both types are important, and can inform each other in useful ways.

However, communities must be intentional in their efforts to focus on both types of youth leadership simultaneously.

3. *Leadership as a position of authority versus leadership as an activity for everyone.* The question of authority and its relationship to youth leadership is highlighted repeatedly throughout this issue. Is leadership exercised only by individuals in positions of authority? Is it possible to be a leader without holding a position of formal authority? Given young people's limited access to positions of authority, this debate has a particular relevance to the study and practice of youth leadership.

4. *"Everyone can be a leader" versus "A select few can be leaders."* Youth leadership scholars and practitioners frequently make implicit assumptions regarding where they stand on this debate. It is a question with important implications for both theory building and program design.

5. *Youth as "future leaders" versus youth as "current leaders."* Should youth leadership programs focus on training young people to become leaders at some future date in some adult context? Or should youth leadership programming view young people as current leaders who are daily exercising power and influence in their communities right now? Again, opinions on this matter are frequently implicit and unexplored, and have important implications for both theory building and program design.

6. *The challenge of youth-adult partnerships in leadership education.* Youth leadership programming inevitably involves relationships between adults and young people. The articles in this issue highlight many of the challenges inherent in managing these relationships: How can adults authentically empower young people? How can adults meaningfully include young people in the decisions that affect their communities? Our contributors share their insights based on their considerable experience negotiating these challenges.

7. *Clarity and alignment in youth leadership education.* Leadership is a challenging issue to explore because it is inherently multifaceted and complex. There are multiple legitimate ways to understand and teach leadership, and different programs appropriately employ different models and pedagogies. In the face of this diversity, two issues become central to the exploration of youth leader-

ship programming. First, is the program clear about the model of leadership it holds at its core? Second, is there alignment between the core model of leadership and the pedagogies used to teach it? In the absence of a single, universal conception of leadership, these two dimensions allow for a meaningful exploration of the theory and practice informing efforts at youth leadership education.

We may not be able to provide simple, easy answers to these debates. However, our contributors have years of experience engaging with the theory and practice of youth leadership and have shown an unmistakable commitment to the importance of this work. We hope that by bringing their voices together in this issue we are bringing new levels of attention, clarity, rigor, and insight to an emerging frontier of interest and inquiry.

We would like to thank all of those who made this work possible. Gil Noam generously offered us the opportunity to edit this issue together, and provided support and guidance in the year that followed. Thanks also to Erin Cooney at the Program in Afterschool Education and Research at Harvard for her help in the final stages of preparation. Finally, thanks to all of the contributors, who took time from their busy lives to share their wisdom with the field through this volume.

Max Klau
Steve Boyd
Lynn Luckow
Editors

MAX KLAU *is senior researcher for leadership and evaluation at City Year in Boston. He received his Ed.D. in June 2005 from the Harvard Graduate School of Education, where he focused his studies on youth leadership.*

STEVE BOYD *is a partner at MacDonald Boyd and Associates, an organizational development and leadership consulting firm based in Seattle, Washington. A founder of the Washington Leadership Institute and the Washington Governor's School for Citizen Leadership, he has been involved in youth leadership education for decades.*

LYNN LUCKOW *consults on strategy and leadership and is currently developing and launching a nationwide Vital Communities Initiative from his base in Northern California. President and CEO of Jossey-Bass Publishers from 1991 to 2000, he later served as president and CEO of Northern California Grantmakers. For ten years (five as chair) he was on the board of trustees of the National 4-H Council, which serves seven million youth annually. During his tenure, ten trustee positions with full voting power were created for youth between ages twelve and twenty-two.*

Executive Summary

Chapter One: The mystery of youth leadership development: The path to just communities
Margaret Libby, Maureen Sedonaen, Steven Bliss

Youth Leadership is clearly relevant to the field of youth development, but it remains remarkably undefined. What exactly is youth leadership? How does the existing literature define it? What do we know for sure about it, and what issues remain unclear or unexplored? In this chapter, the authors review these issues and present the theme of "inside" versus "outside" leadership, suggesting it provides a valuable framework for understanding the challenges of youth leadership.

Chapter Two: Bridging generations: Applying "adult" leadership theories to youth leadership development
Carole A. MacNeil

The subject of adult leadership has long been the focus of intense academic scrutiny. At this point, hundreds of books and dozens of theories examine the dynamics of adult leadership. This chapter explores some simple but crucial questions: *Is youth leadership different from adult leadership? What insights from the literature on adult leadership can we relate to work with youth? What insights are irrelevant or inappropriate?* The author suggests that adult leadership tends to focus on authority (voice, influence, and decision-making power) while youth leadership literature tends to focus on ability (skills, knowledge, and talents). She explores the difference and attempts to bridge the gap.

Chapter Three: Youth leadership and youth development: Connections and questions
Cathann A. Kress

The youth development movement represents a broad trend toward promoting opportunity and resilience over preventing delinquency and failure. Youth leadership, with its inherent focus on positive development, represents a natural area of inquiry for youth development professionals. In this chapter, the author examines the nature of the relationship between the broad youth development movement and the more specific theory and practice of youth leadership. She argues that leadership represents one of the multiple potential developmental pathways for young people. She also takes a clear stand that effective leadership education programs assume that young people are leaders *today*, and should be given meaningful opportunities to practice leadership in a supportive environment.

Chapter Four: Exploring youth leadership in theory and practice: An empirical study
Max Klau

With this chapter we move beyond theoretical and conceptual debates and begin to focus on youth leadership as it is actually understood and practiced in the field. This chapter presents the findings of research involving direct observation of three existing youth leadership programs.

Special Section on youth leadership in action: Key programs and practices

This section brings together the voices of experienced practitioners and the young people with whom they work. Each chapter describes the philosophy and practice of a different type of youth leadership program, and concludes with the voice of a recent participant in the program.

Chapter Five: Leading, learning, and unleashing potential: Youth leadership and civic engagement

Wendy Wheeler, with Carolyn Edlebeck

The author describes the Innovation Center's experience designing and running programming focused on developing youth leadership through civic engagement.

Chapter Six: Moving from "youth leadership development" to "youth in governance": Learning leadership by doing leadership

Carole A. MacNeil with Jennifer McClean

The 4-H program has decades of experience with crafting programs that include young people in local governance. They share their philosophy and experience with crafting these effective youth-adult partnerships.

Chapter Seven: Anytown: NCCJ's youth leadership experience in social justice

Julia Matsudaira with Ashley Jefferson

The NCCJ has extensive experience with designing and running social justice programming for youth. The author describes how this organization develops leadership with a vision of social justice at its core.

Chapter Eight: Arts-Based leadership: Theatrical tributes
Eve Nussbaum Soumarai with Rachel Mazer

The author works with youth to write and perform theatrical tributes to famous historical figures (Anne Frank, Martin Luther King Jr., Nelson Mandela, and others). The process of using the arts to pay tribute to these inspiring people represents another form of youth leadership development.

Resources Guide

In this section, we gather a list of resources for individuals interested in further exploring the programs and concepts presented in this issue.

Some of the mystery around the meaning of youth leadership development, and around what youth leadership means for youth development, can be solved by accounting for the potential connections, as well as the potential tensions and conflicts, between the Inside and Outside approaches.

1

The mystery of youth leadership development: The path to just communities

Margaret Libby, Maureen Sedonaen, Steven Bliss

OUR ORGANIZATION, the Youth Leadership Institute (YLI), was founded in 1989 to address the clear need among youth-serving institutions, such as schools and school districts, community organizations, health care providers and the public health system, and the juvenile justice system, to give young people a real say in the key decisions, programs, and systems that affect them. Over the years, we have promoted both youth leadership and youth development by pushing youth-serving systems and programs to adopt youth development practices and by building youth leadership development pathways inside and outside of those systems in order to achieve better outcomes for young people. To this end, YLI operates a number of community-based civic engagement and leadership development programs, using strategies that include philanthropy, policy advocacy, action research, and organizing, and these programs serve as "learning laboratories" for testing science-based strategies for youth development and youth leadership development. In turn, we capture lessons about strategies and outcomes from these community-based programs, translating them into publications, curricula, and other resources that contribute to the research base on youth development and youth leadership development and that aim to advance the field. Through our national Training Institute, which each year provides more than two hundred trainings, workshops, and presentations, most often to adults in youth-serving systems, we help them create opportunities and pathways for youth to contribute their perspectives and insights toward shaping those systems. We believe that youth have the right to participate in the decision making that affects their lives not only because it provides a key developmental process, but also because the systems in place to address their needs will be better positioned to achieve positive youth outcomes when they have integrated young people into their planning and decision-making processes.

Spanning more than fifteen years, YLI's experience in promoting youth leadership has revealed the importance of working on two fronts to engage youth in creating better systems and communities. We work with groups and decision makers *inside* systems and institutions (that is, schools and government) to educate, inform, and partner with them to map and build an infrastructure that supports inclusive youth participation and leadership and create tools for them to make the process work. We also work with *outside* groups (that is, community coalitions and organizers) to advocate for change on the part of youth-serving systems and communities. It is possible to think of this two-part approach as one that seeks to create change using simultaneously both a "top-down" and a grassroots approach. However, we believe the inside-outside construct is more useful and appropriate, as it places the focus on the systems and communities we seek to transform.

Our "Inside" work includes partnerships across California and the United States with foundations; departments of health, education, juvenile justice, and recreation; as well as city, state, and county municipalities to improve the leadership and engagement opportunities for twelve- to twenty-five-year-olds. Examples of this Inside work include our coordination of the Marin County (California) Youth Commission, which serves as an advisory body to the Marin County Board of Supervisors, and our coordination of the Student Advisory Council, which represents the voice of San Francisco public high school students to the San Francisco Board of Education. An example of our Outside work is the Prevention Youth Councils that YLI staffs in three San Francisco Bay Area counties. These Prevention Youth Councils are youth-led groups that mobilize broad-based community action on alcohol, tobacco, and other youth-related health issues. In both our Inside and Outside work, we have seen the power of institutionalizing pathways for youth to participate in and shape the decision making that affects their lives.

The underlying principle of this chapter is that some of the mystery around the meaning of youth leadership development, and around what youth *leadership* means for youth *development*, can be solved by accounting for the potential connections, as well as the potential tensions and conflicts, between the Inside and Outside approaches. We begin by presenting a brief look back at our nation's legacy of youth civic engagement and a review of the research literature on youth leadership, as a means of setting the context for how youth leadership has traditionally been conceived and to suggest some of the links between the leadership demonstrated in both Inside and Outside efforts. Next, we look at YLI's own experience with three program pathways that support both Inside and Outside strategies, as a means of showing in practice how the two approaches diverge. We then discuss ways in which Inside and Outside approaches to youth leadership need to be cultivated at the levels of individual skills, collective processes, and youth-adult partnerships, and also how lessons from Outside approaches can help imbue Inside approaches with a greater emphasis on action and social justice. We conclude with some thoughts on future research needs on youth leadership through an Inside-Outside lens, and with a challenge to practitioners and policymakers. We believe that looking at the concept of youth leadership within the frame of the Inside-Outside approach helps clarify the goals and strategies of youth leadership development, even as this frame suggests other challenges and questions.

The story of youth leadership thus far: What the research tells us

Youth leadership development is relatively new as an area of study. Yet a look back shows that youth leadership (albeit perhaps not described as such) has not only been a discernable phenomenon in the United States for years but has also been an accepted and celebrated construct woven into the fabric of community life. For years, strategies to transfer knowledge and prepare young people for future roles have been practiced and valued in families, places of worship, clubs, and organizations (for example, Girl Scouts).

Not always transparent or labeled as "leadership development," these opportunities have often been seen as character development, life preparation, and contributing to building relationships and community. Although we do not want to force a strict analogy, it is useful to think of these sorts of youth leadership development as similar to the Inside approach, in the limited sense of occurring within the context of so-called "mainstream," if not dominant, social structures and organizations.

Yet there is also a strong tradition in the United States of youth leading in ways consistent with the Outside model—that is, by acting as advocates from outside the institutions or systems of power. Young people have often been crafting, visioning, and leading social movements, demanding equity and justice.[1] From the civil rights movement and antiwar movements in the 1960s, to the women's rights and environmental movements in the 1970s and

1980s, to the education reform efforts of the 2000s, the energy, talent, passion, and wisdom of young people has demonstrated leadership that is strategic, collective, and powerful. Young people have often been targeted by oppressive rhetoric and policies and scapegoated for "social ills." In spite of this reality, they have often emerged as the crucial frontline leaders doing the work that reframes issues and forces change to occur.

When we look at Inside and Outside strategies within this historical context, the potential fissure and conflict between the two becomes quite clear: Outside strategies are inherently based on contestation and conflict, often calling into the question the values and legitimacy of those inside the systems or organizations, while Inside strategies have not often contributed enough to efforts to transform systems and in some cases have helped to maintain the status quo. While we believe there have been some shortcomings in Inside youth leadership strategies, we also see places where Inside and Outside strategies are working toward common goals, where the approaches could be aligned to move common agendas.

Over the last decade, the research base on youth leadership has defined it in various ways, some focusing on personal characteristics, others on demonstrated actions or processes. Yet, despite the potential rift between Inside and Outside approaches, varying definitions of youth leadership actually provide unifying ways of looking at youth leadership.

One powerful research-based model of youth leadership is that of the "servant leader," adopted by the National Youth Leadership Council. A servant leader is someone who makes decisions that enhance the entire group or organization. Such leaders place high esteem on the values of fairness, integrity, and dependability. They listen to the needs, feedback, and suggestions of all members of the group, not just a select few. Servant leaders view their position as one of responsibility, not ego promotion, and will do the hard work when things get tough. They believe that the group's success is dependent on the work, support, and dedication of all members.[2]

There are two things to highlight about this youth leadership model. First, it could be applied to either Inside or Outside strategies, largely because it concerns advancing group goals, an aim relevant to both types. Second, the servant leader model integrates individual *traits* as well as collective *processes*.

If we look at other models of leadership, drawn from research on community organizing and community youth development, we again see this intersection of traits and processes, which is crucial in that it ultimately relates to how we can deliberately promote youth leadership. Leadership is defined in three such models as follows (one model focuses specifically on youth leadership):

- An endeavor that emphasizes the developmental areas of leading and connecting and includes training in skills such as self-advocacy and conflict resolution; exposure to personal leadership and youth development activities, including community service; and opportunities that allow youth to exercise leadership.
- "The ability to guide or direct others on a course of action, influence the opinion and behavior of other people, and show the way by going in advance."[3]
- Organizations in communities that focus on youth leadership and youth voice. Youth provide leadership and direction, taking a central role in designing activities, establishing and enforcing formal and informal rules for members.[4]

Again, we want to highlight that research-based models of leadership, and youth leadership in particular, help us think about leadership holistically—that is, as something that cuts across the Inside-Outside divide. At the same time, examining the distinctions between the Inside and Outside approaches helps us understand how they can each be promoted, what their respective strengths are, and how we can create linkages between the two. As a way of starting to tease that "whole" apart, we look now at three of YLI's core strategies in promoting youth leadership, and how these strategies diverge in the Inside and Outside contexts.

Philanthropy, action research, and policy advocacy: Three proven pathways

YLI over the years has implemented and tested various models for youth leadership, seeking to create and refine pathways for youth to take on progressively more sophisticated and challenging leadership roles over time. We have found three models to be especially promising in creating pathways for youth to participate in community priority setting, problem solving, and decision making. These models are youth philanthropy, evaluation and action research, and policy advocacy. Here we look at each of these pathways and discuss their applicability via Inside and Outside strategies.

Youth philanthropy

At YLI, *youth philanthropy* involves youth receiving training and support to make decisions about what youth-led projects to fund. In addition to helping young people serve as grant makers, youth philanthropy enables young people to serve as *grant seekers*, with an opportunity to lead projects, from design to implementation to evaluation, with support from adult allies. As an Inside approach to youth leadership, YLI's youth philanthropy area includes the Philanthropy Learning Network, a program that links adult philanthropists with young people who participate in youth philanthropy programs in the San Francisco Bay Area. Philanthropy Learning Network, in addition to enabling adult and youth philanthropists to learn from one another, seeks to create decision-making roles for youth within philanthropic organizations. At the same time, youth philanthropy at YLI paves the way for Outside approaches. As grant seekers, youth leaders can obtain funds for projects that might not be funded otherwise, such as youth-led grassroots activism focused on systems and policy change.

Evaluation and action research

At YLI, youth-led *evaluation and action research* (EAR) involves training and supporting youth to design and carry out research that will inform their action, whether it is the development of education campaigns, policy advocacy, or recommendations for program improvement. It provides youth with an opportunity to develop data-driven ideas and recommendations, which gives them credibility when offering recommendations to and making demands of local decision makers. Often youth researchers are collecting data that illuminate issues in new ways, as they are able to design surveys and conduct focus groups in ways that better reach their peers than those designed by adults. An example of EAR as an Inside strategy would be local data-gathering undertaken by the Marin County (California) Youth Commission in creating recommendations for the Marin County Board of Supervisors, or the various youth-led program evaluations facilitated by YLI. At the same time, through its recently launched GIRL Project, YLI is helping young women in two San Francisco Bay Area counties to gather data that will form the basis for advocating for new, more effective approaches to meeting young women's health needs.

Policy advocacy

YLI's *policy advocacy* work involves training and preparing youth to create, adapt, or enforce policies. It provides youth advocates with opportunities to lead efforts to bring youth perspectives and experiences into the policymaking arena, in order to make policies that better address youth needs and achieve youth outcomes. YLI supports a number of policy advocacy projects that take an Inside approach, such as the Marin County Youth Commission and the Student Advisory Council in San Francisco. As an Outside policy advocacy strategy, YLI's three Prevention Youth Councils throughout the Bay Area seek to mobilize community coalitions that advocate for policies that address alcohol, tobacco, and other drug (ATOD) use and abuse among youth, and other public health challenges on the local level.

Through these three leadership pathways, youth are taking action to improve their schools, communities, programs, and communities. These models seek to institutionalize the training and support that youth leaders need to be effective, by working from either outside or inside those institutions and systems. Like the research base on leadership models, these pathways help us to see commonalities across Inside and Outside approaches to youth leadership development. Yet the examples of Inside and Outside strategies help us understand the distinct differences between seeking to create change within a system and from outside a system. Take the examples in youth-led EAR. Whereas the Marin County Youth Commission has an established mechanism for getting its findings and recommendations heard in the policymaking arena, via its role as an advisory body to the Marin County Board of Supervisors, participants in the GIRL Project will need to use media advocacy, community organizing, and other means to get on the "radar screen" of policymakers and other decision makers. These differences are more than theoretical. The differences between Inside and Outside strategies have real implications for how practitioners of youth development and youth leadership, as well as adult allies, must work to support these approaches.

A learning agenda, part one: What inside can learn from outside

In the Outside approach to youth leadership, the idea of a power imbalance is taken for granted: those working from the inside have it; those working from the outside do not, that is, until they organize. Practitioners using Inside approaches can be more vigilant in acknowledging and addressing the ways that power relations influence youth leadership and youth development.

Power is a concept that is often used in the youth development field in the context of inspiring young people to "be empowered" or "feel your own sense of power." It is often assumed that leaders are people with power and vice versa, that is, the more power we have, the more success we will have as a leader. These notions of power can lead to confusion when adults take steps to empower or share power with young people. In supporting youth leadership, it is key for practitioners to try to utilize positive youth-adult partnerships as a strategy to build leadership skills through mentoring and shared power. As partners in leadership, ideally young people and adults come together to plan, problem solve, learn, and strengthen their relationships with each other and in the community. It is important for practitioners to be aware of and to address the ongoing role that power dynamics play as they build and sustain power-sharing relationships and structures with young people.[5] At the core of successful youth-adult partnerships to build leadership is a transference and creation of shared power—an implied equality of responsibility, accountability, and control.[6]

Since young people have been left out of the process and without true decision-making power around issues that directly and indirectly impact them, many of our efforts in creating youth-adult partnerships have attempted to create settings where both youth and adult voices can be heard on an equal level, with a reciprocal value to each participant's contribution. These efforts aimed at sharing the vocal power, although intended to produce and support equity, often fall short—because we have not truly dissected the factors that have led to power inequities in these partnerships, nor have we accepted the true depth of young people as leaders.[7]

In emulating the Outside's explicit attention to power imbalances, Inside approaches must also be clear about creating an even playing field *among* youth. Just as in adult society, access to power occurs through the filters of race, class, gender, sexual orientation, and ability. These factors often influence which youth are already succeeding within the systems, and it is these youth who have traditionally been sought as leaders in Inside strategies. Youth leadership development practitioners must therefore, as a matter of equity, explore how to create more opportunities for marginalized youth to participate in priority setting, problem solving, and decision making through Inside settings. Youth whose needs have not been met by their schools, communities, and other youth-serving systems have an expertise that is critical to transforming those institutions. Failing to engage traditionally marginalized youth means we are missing out on the insights and expertise that these youth have to contribute, and also means that communities that would most benefit from capacity building and youth leadership development are not being supported or included. In terms of the longer-term impact (that is, what happens to youth leaders when they grow up), we have seen many Inside youth leaders go on to a variety of careers while Outside youth leaders often continue to do work that reflects their social justice values.

In short, what Inside approaches ultimately can learn from Outside approaches, through a focus on power structures and marginalized populations, is a commitment to the value of social justice. A full definition of youth leadership must encompass values, power, and action; without power sharing, a theory of change, and action, youth are not exercising leadership, but taking steps to plan and implement activities prescribed by adults.

A learning agenda, part two: Where more research is needed

There is little research about youth leadership development generally and in particular about the relationship between it and social justice and the outcomes achieved when these concepts are paired to drive collective action. Here the authors outline a set of youth leadership development topics that would benefit from further inquiry:

- Components of effective youth leadership development practice
- How practitioners prepare and support marginalized youth to participate in Inside and Outside leadership development
- How to use a youth-adult partnership approach toward making systems change
- How to infuse social justice values and structures into Inside youth leadership activities
- How to use youth leadership development strategies to address inequity in youth outcomes
- What conditions, structures, and practices support sustainable youth engagement in systems change

A challenge to organizations and practitioners

Youth leadership development pathways can contribute to efforts to push the youth development field to incorporate social-justice-based values into its vision for youth and communities. They also can push the field to integrate new kinds of skills and preparation into the existing frameworks to provide youth with the tools they need to transform youth-serving systems and societal institutions, and to address inequity. This shift means adopting a new view and practice concerning youth and the role they play in community priority setting, problem solving, and decision making. We challenge the field to consider the notion that more leadership roles for youth within the field is central not just to creating quality programs, settings, systems, communities, and a society that truly values and invests in young people, but to our shared goal of just communities. Without youth participation and leadership, we cannot achieve good outcomes for all young people. There are serious issues we need to address: the achievement gap, criminalization of young people, obesity, increasing poverty, and reduced local, state, and national budgets. In this time of scarce resources and growing challenges, it is ever more critical to allocate resources toward not just youth development, but specifically youth leadership development and to ensure that we are targeting those resources toward youth from communities where these resources are sorely needed. Additionally, practitioners working on the Inside and Outside must begin dialogues and identify places where their agendas overlap, rather than compete. These conversations will surely reveal common goals and produce new and creative strategies to strengthen our efforts to transform youth-serving institutions and programs and communities, in order to achieve good outcomes for all young people.

Notes

1. Mohamed, I., & Wheeler, W. (2001). *Broadening the bounds of youth development: Youth as engaged citizens.* Chevy Chase, MD: The Innovation Center and the Ford Foundation.

2. Spears, L. (1998). *Tracing the impact of servant leadership. Insights on leadership*. New York: Wiley.
3. Wehmeyer, M. L., Agran, M., & Hughes, C. (1998). *Teaching self-determination to students with disabilities.*Baltimore: Brookes Publishing.
4. McLaughlin, M. (2000). *Community counts: How organizations matter for youth development.* Washington, DC: Public Education Network.
5. Sedonaen, M., Rowles, E., & Aung, K. (2003). *Contextualizing power: An introductory approach to the roles of race and class in youth adult partnerships.* Chevy Chase, MD: Innovation Center for Community and Youth Development and the National 4H Council.
6. Libby, M., Rosen, M., & Sedonaen, M. (2005). Building youth-adult partnerships for community change: Lessons from the Youth Leadership Institute. *Journal of Community Psychology, 33*(1), 111–120.
7. Roach, C., Cao Yu, H., & Lewis-Charp, H. (1998). Race, poverty and youth development. *Poverty & Race*, July/August 2001; Lynch, E., & Hanson, M. (1998). *Developing cross-cultural competence: A guide for working with children and their families* (2nd ed.). Baltimore: Brookes Publishing.

MARGARET LIBBY, *senior director of research at YLI, leads YLI's research and evaluation work at the statewide and local levels and YLI's youth evaluation and action research projects.*

MAUREEN SEDONAEN, *Youth Leadership Institute (YLI) founder and president, is a nationally recognized authority in the fields of youth leadership and youth development.*

STEVEN BLISS, *writer, researcher, and consultant specializing in youth development, urban planning, community development, and public health, has consulted to YLI on fund development, communications, and program planning since 2001.*

The vast literature related to adult leadership has very little to say about youth leadership. Adult leadership literature tends to focus on issues of authority (voice, influence, and decision-making power). In contrast, youth leadership literature tends to focus on issues of ability (skills, knowledge, and talents). The author explores the difference and attempts to bridge the gap.

2

Bridging generations: Applying "adult" leadership theories to youth leadership development

Carole A. MacNeil

FOR NEARLY A CENTURY, leadership scholars have attempted to define the concepts of "leadership" and "leader" and to understand the essential attributes, functions, and circumstances that characterize effective leaders.[1] However, "despite tens of thousands of pages written about it, leadership remains an elusive concept."[2] Early research on leadership focused on the qualities and traits of the "leader" rather than the process of leadership. These "great-man theories" were popular in the early 1900s and attempted to identify some unique, and perhaps mysterious, qualities of leaders.[3] The great-man theories emphasized inherent qualities or the social position of an individual, with the underlying assumption that leaders are born, not made; that a person is "naturally" a leader, rather than educated into leadership roles. Similarly, trait theories focused on those unique characteristics that qualify a person for leadership. This approach focused on the ways that leaders are different from "other" individuals, and attempted to identify the core traits that qualify a person for leadership and contribute to his or her effectiveness in that role.

As leadership theories continued to develop in the early- to mid-twentieth century, the focus shifted from the individual to the group or organization.[4] This work focused on the contexts and particular circumstances of leadership, how the leader's traits, group function, and specific context affect the leader's effectiveness. Later in the twentieth century, "psychoanalytic" and "behavioral" theories appeared; the former looked at why people are motivated to lead, or to follow a particular leader; the latter drew from psychology to examine the ways that positive or negative reinforcement could be used by leaders to motivate followers and influence behavior.[5] In the mid- to late-twentieth century, the literature began to reflect more focus on exchange theories and was influenced by management sciences.[6]

A more modern trend in leadership theory is the movement away from the concept of leadership residing in one person, toward a concept of leadership residing in the relationship between and among individuals.[7] For example, Bolman and Deal suggest that leadership exists only in a relationship and is dependent on the perceptions of the persons involved in that relationship.[8] Both leaders and followers shape the relationship and the leadership functions. Within this construct, leadership no longer resides in the person and thus is not dependent on a leadership position.

The evolution of leadership theory, however, is by no means linear. It is still possible to see the evidence of trait theories or even "great man" thinking in contemporary writing on leadership. For the purposes of this exploration, I propose a working definition of leadership that draws from contemporary leadership theories, the literature on leadership development, and studies of applied leadership:

Leadership is a relational process combining ability (knowledge, skills, and talents) with authority (voice, influence, and decision-making power) to positively influence and impact diverse individuals, organizations, and communities.

This definition incorporates the contextual nature of leadership, shaped by the relationships within a particular leadership context[9] and the concept of diversity as a key issue and opportunity for leaders.[10] The definition also acknowledges the applied nature of leadership (that is, that leadership is evidenced in the act of leading: having authority, not simply ability), an important consideration in the comparison between writings about adult versus youth leadership. More detail about these concepts will be presented later in this chapter.

Presence (and absence) of youth in the leadership literature

To explore the relationship between youth and adult leadership—or the relationship between the youth leadership literature and the adult leadership literature—it is important to examine where and how youth appear in the discussions on leadership. Where are youth present in the leadership literature? Likewise, where is leadership present in the youth literature?

In the "tens of thousands of pages" written about leadership, what are the contributions to our understanding of youth leadership, youth leadership development, and the differences between youth and adult leadership? In much of the literature focused on leadership theory, leadership development, or leadership practice, youth are noticeably absent. For example, in a comprehensive review conducted by Bass of more than five thousand leadership studies, there is nothing about youth as leaders or about leadership development for youth.[11] The leadership literature, both popular and scholarly, focuses heavily on adult leadership development and practice.

Where young people are referenced, it is frequently with a future orientation. That is, the focus is on the need to begin working with young people now so they can develop the skills they will need to be effective leaders later (presumably, when they are adults).

For example, in his important work *On Leadership*, Gardner speaks to the importance of developing leadership potential in youth. While he lays out a plan for youth leadership development, it is with the underlying assumption that youth will learn now but practice later.[12] Similarly, O'Connell calls for increased attention to leadership development (that is, preparing youth now so they can lead later).[13]

This call for attention to leadership development, and the need to focus on youth as well as adults, is also found in some of the leadership literature focused on educational contexts. These studies, focused on both higher education and secondary education, suggest that effective leadership is a critical issue in contemporary society, and one that can and should be addressed by education.[14]

The field of youth development, and the increasing body of research in the field, has also contributed to arguments for the need for youth leadership development, often emphasizing how those learning experiences might be structured, implemented, and measured. Within this context of youth development, youth leadership development can be defined as "the provision of experiences, from highly structured to quite informal, that help young people develop [a set of competencies that allow young people to lead others over the long term]."[15] However, in the youth or adolescent literature that addresses the need for youth leadership development, the conceptual framework guiding this "provision of experiences" can range from a deficit model of youth (that is, a set of problems to fix) to a model of youth as resources (that is, offering unique contributions to their organizations and communities).[16]

Many of the arguments for doing youth leadership development are framed in terms similar to arguments for youth programs in general: that is, in terms of intervention or prevention of risky behaviors. Youth leadership development can be framed as a way of providing interventions for youth who are facing particular challenges or are already engaged in risky behaviors, or it can be framed as a prevention strategy, helping to provide opportunities that prevent youth from engaging in risky behaviors. From a positive youth development perspective, leadership development experiences are good for all youth, providing them with supportive relationships and opportunities to see themselves (and be seen by others) as having valuable contributions to make to the world. Further, their active engagement can help them develop self-esteem, confidence, and essential social and intellectual competencies[17] and can provide an important foundation for future civic involvement.[18]

While this is certainly a worthwhile goal, these approaches don't fully capitalize on the power and potential of youth leadership development to benefit not only the youth participants but also the organization and communities in which young people practice leadership. Some youth development and leadership researchers suggest a different framework, one that focuses on the role of youth as problem solvers, not problems to be solved; youth as assets to communities, not liabilities. These researchers have made the call to rethink youth leadership development as something beneficial to society as a whole[19] and to see youth for what they have to offer, not just what they need.[20]

Regardless of the rationale, the literature on youth leadership development focuses heavily on defining the essential components for a leadership program, or on the specific programs and activities that can help youth develop their leadership skills and knowledge. This focus on skills and knowledge highlights an important distinction between the literature about youth and the literature about adults, discussed in the rest of this chapter.

Leadership development and the presence of ability and authority

Based on a comparison of the literature focused on adult leadership development compared to the leadership literature focused on youth (or the youth development literature focused on leadership), an important contrast comes into focus. The literature addressing youth leadership development most often focuses on leadership *ability* (skills, knowledge, and talents): for example, how do, and how should, educators support youth in development of specific leadership skills? By contrast, the adult leadership literature may address ability, but it also focuses on issues of *authority* (voice, influence, and decision-making power): how do, and how should, leaders apply those skills to real-life situations where significant consequences are at stake?

There are many reasons for this difference in framing leadership for adults versus leadership for youth, but one of the most salient may be the way youth are "framed" in our society. Youth in general in this culture, and in particular youth who have been labeled "at risk" or who have been identified as needing extra resources for their positive development, can be limited by the very labels ostensibly meant to support their growth.[21] Public discourse presents certain youth as "at risk," damaged or dysfunctional. In particular, "adolescents are supposed to be rebellious, defiant of adult authority, moody, unmanageable, high risk-takers with no thought of the future, alienated, and so on."[22]

Similarly, Giroux speaks to this limited (and limiting) construction of youth: "While 'youth' as a social construction has always been mediated, in part, as a social problem, many cultural critics believe that postmodern youth are uniquely 'alien,' 'strange,' and disconnected from the real world."[23] Within this definition of youth, it is easy to understand why the focus of youth leadership development would be on ability, and would not only overlook but intentionally avoid considerations of authority. Even many youth development programs—those entities created to support and advocate for youth—are explicitly or implicitly grounded in a public health model, which "identifies, isolates, and then treats the subject in order to restore him or her to good health, meaning adjustment into mainstream or dominant culture."[24]

This negative construction of the meaning of youth is a form of oppression, referred to as either ageism or "adultism."[25] Not only does one group (adults) have the power to construct the definition of another group (youth), but they also have the power to act on those definitions, to create structures that reinforce and reconfirm the very beliefs they have constructed. Adultism can be a tremendous obstacle for youth leadership development.[26]

The result of adultism is that youth (particularly adolescence) is seen as a problem time, to be suffered through, rather than as a positive stage of life development. Young people, then, are silenced and "warehoused" in schools or youth programs until they are old enough to join society. Clearly, this attitude is not one that encourages either young people or adults to see youth as being organizational or community leaders.

Finding a place for youth in the adult leadership literature

If the youth leadership literature is mostly silent about important aspects of leadership development and practice—such as issues of voice, influence, and decision-making power (or "authority")—what would the adult leadership literature, with a dual focus on ability and authority, have to tell us about youth leadership? Where in the leadership literature might we find guidance for our work in youth leadership development?

First, the adult leadership literature suggests that leadership is learned and honed in the context of practicing leadership. The focus is on learning, and applying, new skills and knowledge in real-life contexts. If youth programs are seeking to support youth in developing leadership, the leadership literature suggests that we must frame our programs so that youth have opportunities not only to develop skills and knowledge but also to apply them in meaningful and authentic ways. By "meaningful" I refer to decisions that have true impact and consequences; by "authentic" I refer to real decisions that need to be made for the organization or community, rather than simulations or "mock" situations—in short, the kinds of decisions that adult leaders must make every day.

Second, if we are talking about authentic and meaningful leadership roles for youth within a societal context where youth are marginalized and where adults hold the power, then we are talking about a critical role for adults in creating those authentic and meaningful roles. For youth to develop and practice leadership, adults will have to share power, and this renegotiation of power is fraught with challenges. But some of the literature on adult leadership can assist our understanding of how to proceed. The literature that focuses on issues of diversity can help us frame the relationships between youth and adults (with age being an important facet of diversity). The literature focusing on functional approaches to leadership can assist us in our thinking about power imbalances and what gets accomplished (and by whom). The literature on collaborative leadership can help us think more about the contexts in which leadership is practiced, and how to make those contexts more inclusive for a wide range of leaders and leadership styles (including youth).

Leadership and diversity intersect in different ways and in different contexts. Demographic changes, job mobility, and other forms of social mobility within the United States mean that settings of all types are being affected by population changes. Many leadership scholars underscore the importance of diversity as a factor of leadership in a wide range of contexts.[27] These scholars and others make the case that diversity is not only inevitable but also desirable. Diversity within a leadership context leads to better decision making[28] and more unified visions for the future.[29] Some literature also suggests that effective leadership understands and actively addresses issues of diversity, and in so doing, counters patterns of inequality in U.S. society.[30]

The rationales for seeking and the strategies for supporting diverse leadership may be useful to youth leadership scholars in framing rationales and strategies for supporting youth in both learning and practicing leadership. How does the integration of youth into authentic leadership roles benefit not only the youth but also the adults and organizations? How are the organizations or communities' outcomes enhanced by the leadership roles of young people? Just as the research on diversity has examined the positive effects on organizational outcomes, the research on youth will need to look at how a diversity of ages within leadership contexts can and does affect organizational or community outcomes. There is some evidence from the youth development literature that when youth are engaged in authentic opportunities for leadership (where they not only develop their leadership abilities but also exercise leadership authority), their leadership has a real impact, either on their organization or on a specific project.[31] In some cases, this engagement focuses on a specific social issue or cause (such as neighborhood revitalization);[32] in others, it focuses on the accomplishment of a group goal (such as creating a public performance).[33] Still, more research on organizational or community outcomes is needed if there is to be a shift from the concept of youth leadership as "good for youth" to a concept of youth integration into leadership roles as "good for all."

In functional frameworks of leadership, scholars focus on identifying the functions of the leadership process rather than on the characteristics of the leader. This discussion may take the form of morale versus task functions,[34] or group maintenance versus achievement of group goals,[35] or concern for people versus concern for tasks.[36] Some scholars have used a feminist framework to explore the connection between these relational, morale functions and socially constructed gender roles. Within this framework, task functions are of a higher status and become synonymous with "leadership," while the morale functions (typically performed by women) are of less status and not seen as part of leadership. For example, in Astin and Leland's study of seventy-seven women leaders—all highly successful in terms of process and outcomes—"effective leadership" meant shared power and collective action.[37] In the model of leadership emerging from this study, the leader was not at the top of some hierarchy, dictating orders, but rather functioning as a facilitator of group processes, helping the group reach its goal.

For youth leadership scholars, this functional-feminist framework may help us rethink the ways we might study youth leadership development. Likewise, for youth leadership development practitioners, it might suggest a different way of defining and practicing leadership, so that leadership can be shared across functions rather than residing in one person (for example, the youth worker). This functional approach, with its emphasis on relationships among group members, may also have particular implications for young people at specific periods of development, that is, when relationships with peers peak in importance, including those relationships formed and maintained through specific leadership experiences.[38]

There is also a significant body of scholarship on collaborative leadership, which often connects in important ways with discussions on diversity or functional-feminist frameworks of leadership. Many scholars argue that changing social contexts and conditions require a more collaborative framework for understanding and practicing leadership.[39] For example, Rost suggests that the industrial leadership paradigm (identified by such characteristics as a "personalistic focus on the leader," a "self-interested and individualistic outlook," and a "male model of life") is insufficient to serve the needs of contemporary and future society.[40] A postindustrial model will need to incorporate values such as collaboration, diversity in organizational structures and activities, and a "consensus-oriented policy-making process."[41] Ken Torp and Lisa Carlson point to a relatively recent shift from the leader as an issuer of commands to a person who needs and seeks the participation and input of "followers."[42] They suggest that this paradigm shift is linked to civil rights movements, in which marginalized groups began to gain a voice and power over their own lives and decisions.

While this shift is by no means absolute, it does create openings for marginalized groups to participate more fully in leadership processes. Perhaps these openings can be created for youth as well. By looking at the research on collaborative leadership, such as Chrislip and Larson's study of fifty-two successful collaborative initiatives, youth leadership professionals may be able to identify strategies for effectively incorporating young people into leadership processes, and for addressing the power issues and imbalances that inevitably arise in collaborative structures (including those power imbalances between youth and adults).

The hard, but critical, work of bridge building

The leadership literature focused on adults suggests that incorporating diversity (including diverse ages) or developing more collaborative, functional approaches to leadership (where leadership is shared among group members, including youth and adults) is neither straightforward nor easy. And while there is much to suggest that developing youth leadership is important for youth, adults, and their organizations and communities, there are still many questions about how this can be accomplished most effectively. Simply inviting youth to be a part of the "leadership team" doesn't mean that young people will come away with a self-concept of "leader" or improved leadership skills, or that they will have had opportunities to influence the group's direction or make decisions. The presence of youth in community or organizational processes does not necessarily indicate that a transformation of power dynamics, or even an examination of current power relationships, will occur. In reality, whether one looks at the contexts of school, youth-serving organizations, or communities, rarely are young people involved in decision making or creation of policy, except perhaps in token ways.

Earlier I suggested the following working definition of leadership:

Leadership is a relational process combining ability (knowledge, skills, and talents) with authority (voice, influence, and decision-making power) to positively influence and impact diverse individuals, organizations, and communities.

The adult leadership development literature would suggest that a dual focus on ability (learning) and authority (doing) is critical for successful leadership. By contrast, the youth leadership development literature more often focuses on learning about leadership, but not necessarily on the application of that learning to authentic, meaningful activities. "Authority" is often missing in this youth developmental focus. While it is certainly important to understand how youth develop leadership skills and self-concepts, without a concurrent examination of authority issues (that is, how young people come to have voice and to practice decision making), one could argue that young people are simply learning *about* leadership rather than learning leadership, that they are developing an understanding of leadership without opportunities to practice it. Bringing youth into leadership processes in their schools, communities, organizations, or other groups is not only good for those youth who are involved, but also has benefits for the adults and the larger organization. Zeldin and Camino suggest that youth leadership development can serve multiple purposes: it is simultaneously an end in itself by promoting healthy youth development and a means to an end as youth make contributions through their participation.[43] Tapping into the insights, talents, and energies of young people can help groups and communities develop and implement more effective solutions to issues.[44] An analysis of evaluations done of sixty-nine youth programs showed that not only do youth respond positively to opportunities to make a positive difference, but they also are capable of making significant contributions to their communities.[45] Young people have perspectives and experience that adults do not. Given that, they have important insights that can benefit the group in developing solutions to problems and in achieving its goals.[46] This argument can be extended to suggest not only that young people's contributions are useful, but also that their energy, knowledge, talents, and skills are critical in solving the challenges faced by modern-day organizations and communities.

Conclusion

Is there a significant difference between youth and adult leadership? There is certainly a difference between the literature focused on adult leadership and the literature focused on youth leadership. But does that mean there is a difference between the leadership practices of young people and the leadership practices of adults? The question itself assumes a singular definition of "youth" and "adults" (and perhaps of "leadership"). Using a framework of diversity and functional leadership as discussed earlier, I would suggest that there are significant differences in the needs, styles, and practices of leaders, depending on a host of cultural or identity factors (including age). But age does not stand alone; youth, like adults, are unique combinations of age, ethnicity, gender, sexual orientation, life experience, and other factors.

Leadership needs, styles, and practices may also vary greatly on the basis of previous leadership experiences. Certainly the leadership style and needs of a sixth-grade class president, for example, will be significantly different from those of a college student protesting the college's hiring practices. Developmental factors play a role in this, as do the leadership demands of the particular context. However, while adults (presumably) have had more time and opportunities to develop their leadership skills, it is not necessarily the case that increases in age correlate with higher levels of leadership skills. While one's leadership may be influenced by processes of human development (the leader's "stage" of development), it is also influenced by one's individual pathway of leadership development. It is quite possible that a nineteen-year-old may have more significant leadership experience than a thirty-nine-year-old. In other words, developmental stage alone cannot serve as an indicator or guideline for youth leadership development. Youth, like adults, will practice leadership based on their particular developmental stage and leadership experience. In short, leadership scholars and youth leadership educators would not be well served to adopt a linear model of leadership development that is completely age dependent. Rather, our thinking about youth leadership development may be better informed by a broader, more contextual approach that incorporates the unique experiences of the individual, the larger context of the leadership practice, and the specific opportunities for voice, influence, and decision making.

The differences in youth and adult leadership may also be based on other factors, including the policies and procedures of the context in which leadership is being practiced. The degree to which individuals can practice leadership will be shaped by the organizational and political context and by the implicit or explicit rules that govern that context. For example, youth members of boards of directors or similar decision-making bodies may not be allowed to participate fully because of the group's bylaws, traditions, or underlying assumptions about who gets a "vote."

The wealth of scholarly work on leadership development can be tremendously useful to youth leadership educators. First, its broad range of exploration about essential leadership skills and knowledge (what I have referred to as the "ability" side of leadership) can help inform our thinking about how particular skills characterize, and enhance, effective leadership. Second, the theoretical base examining adult leadership reveals a component missing from much of the youth leadership literature: opportunities for developing and practicing voice, influence, and decision making (or what I have referred to as the "authority" aspect of leadership). The reasons for the omission are many, but so are the opportunities for youth leadership development when the omission is brought to light. If leadership development is learned in the "doing," how might youth leadership efforts be enhanced when youth have authentic opportunities to "do" leadership?

Those working in youth leadership development might be challenged and motivated to think about how to incorporate voice, influence, and decision-making power (not simply skills) into their work with youth. Likewise, leadership scholars might contribute to the thinking about youth leadership development by studying youth leadership in action; what are the outcomes of those contexts and processes in which youth not only are learning about leadership and developing leadership skills and knowledge, but also are truly practicing leadership by influencing and affecting individuals, organizations, and communities? The opportunities for youth leadership practitioners and scholars to learn from the adult leadership literature are many; the greatest challenge to doing so may be our own limitations in thinking about youth and their capacity for leadership. However, the benefits—to youth, their organizations, and communities—of doing so make it worth the effort.

Notes

1. Bass, B. (1981). *Stogdill's handbook of leadership.* New York: Free Press. Rost, J. (1991). *Leadership for the twenty-first century.* Westport, CT: Praeger.
2. Bolman, L., & Deal, T. (1991). *Reframing organizations: Artistry, choice, and leadership.* San Francisco: Jossey-Bass, p. 404.
3. Bass. (1981).
4. Rost. (1991).
5. Bass. (1981).
6. Rost. (1991).
7. Astin, H., & Leland, C. (1991). *Women of influence, women of vision: A cross-generational study of leaders and social change.* San Francisco: Jossey-Bass. Bolman & Deal. (1991). Helgesen, S. (1995). *The female advantage: Women's ways of leadership.* New York: Currency Doubleday. Hope, A., & Timmel, S. (1984). *Training for transformation: A handbook for community workers.* Zimbabwe: Mambo Press.
8. Bolman & Deal. (1991).
9. Astin & Leland. (1991). DePree, M. (1989). *Leadership is an art.* New York: Dell. Hesselbein, F. (2002). *Hesselbein on leadership.* San Francisco: Jossey-Bass.
10. Melendez, S. (1996). An "outsider's" view of leadership. In F. Hesselbein, M. Goldsmith, & R. Beckhard (Eds.), *The leader of the future.* San Francisco: Jossey-Bass. Offermann, L. (1997). Leading and empowering diverse followers. In Leadership and Followership Focus Group (Ed.), *The balance of leadership and followership.* College Park, MD: Kellogg Leadership Studies Project. Work, J. (1996). Leading a diverse work force. In F. Hesselbein, M. Goldsmith, and R. Beckhard (Eds.), *The leader of the future.* San Francisco: Jossey-Bass.
11. Bass. (1981).
12. Gardner, J. (1990). *On leadership.* New York: Free Press.
13. O'Connell, B. (1994). *People power: Service, advocacy, empowerment.* New York: Foundation Center.
14. Higher Education Research Institute. (1996). *A social change model of leadership development.* Los Angeles: University of California. Nemerowicz, G., & Rosi, E. (1997). *Education for leadership and social responsibility.* London: Falmer Press.
15. Zeldin, S., & Camino, L. (1999). Youth leadership: Linking research and program theory to exemplary practice. *New Designs for Youth Development, 15*(1), 10–15, p. 11.
16. MacNeil, C. (2000). *Youth-adult collaborative leadership: Strategies for fostering ability and authority.* Michigan: UMI Dissertation Services.
17. Hechinger, F. (1992). *Fateful choices.* New York: Carnegie Council on Adolescent Development. Lakes, R. (1996). *Youth development and critical education: The promise of democratic action.* New York: SUNY Press. McLaughlin, M., Irby, M., & Langman, J. (1994). *Urban sanctuaries: Neighborhood organizations in the lives and futures of inner-city youth.* San Francisco: Jossey-Bass. Takanishi, R. (1993). Changing views of adolescence in contemporary society. In R. Takanishi (Ed.), *Adolescence in the 1990s: Risk and opportunity.* New York: Teachers College Press.
18. Independent Sector. (2002). *Engaging youth in lifelong service.* Washington, DC: Independent Sector.

19. Olson, J., Goddard, H., Solheim, C., & Sandt, L. (2004). Making a case for engaging adolescents in program decision-making. *Journal of Extension, 42*(6). Zeldin & Camino. (1999).

20. Benson, P. (1997). *All kids are our kids: What communities must do to raise caring and responsible children and adolescents.* San Francisco: Jossey-Bass. Kretzmann, J., & McKnight, J. (1993). *Building communities from the inside out: A path toward finding and mobilizing a community's assets.* Evanston, IL: Center for Urban Affairs and Policy Research. Lakes. (1996). MacNeil, C., & Krensky, B. (1996). A Project YES case study: Who are the real service providers? *Education and Urban Society, 28*(2), 176–188. Smith, R. (1997). Introduction. In American Youth Policy Forum (Ed.), *Some things DO make a difference for youth: A compendium of evaluations of youth programs and practices.* Washington, DC: American Youth Policy Forum. Zeldin, S., Camino, L., & Calvert, M. (2003). Toward an understanding of youth in community governance: Policy priorities and research directions. *Social Policy Report, 17*(3).

21. Kretzmann & McKnight. (1993). Medoff, P., & Sklar, H. (1994). *Streets of hope: The fall and rise of an urban neighborhood.* Boston, MA: South End Press.

22. Takanishi. (1993). p. 2.

23. Giroux, H. (1996). Doing cultural studies: Youth and the challenge of pedagogy. In P. Leistyna, A. Woodrum, & S. Sherblom (Eds.), *Breaking free: The transformative power of critical pedagogy* (p. 90). Reprint Series number 27. Cambridge, MA: Harvard Educational Review.

24. Lakes. (1996). p. 17.

25. Checkoway, B., & Richards-Schuster, K. (2001). Young people as agents of community change: New lessons from the field. *PPFY Network, 4*(2). Stoneman, D. (1993). *Leadership development: A handbook from YouthBuild USA and the Youth Action Program.* Somerville, MA: YouthBuild USA.

26. Lakes. (1996).

27. For example, Clifton, R., & Dahms, A. (1993). *Grassroots organizations.* Prospect Heights, IL: Waveland Press. Melendez. (1996). Offermann. (1997). Work. (1996).

28. Lakey, B., Lakey, G., Napier, R., & Robinson, J. (1995). *Grassroots and nonprofit leadership: A guide for organizations in changing times.* Philadelphia: New Society. Offermann. (1997).

29. Melendez. (1996).

30. Hesselbein. (2002). Nemerowicz & Rosi. (1997). Lakey et al. (1995).

31. Lakes. (1996). McLaughlin et al. (1994). Zeldin & Camino. (1999). Zeldin, S. (2004). Youth as agents of adult and community development: Mapping the processes and outcomes of youth engaged in organizational governance. *Applied Developmental Science, 8*(2), 75–90.

32. Medoff & Sklar. (1994).

33. In McLaughlin et al. (1994).

34. Kokopeli, B., & Lakey, G. (n.d.). *Leadership for change: Toward a feminist model.* Santa Cruz, CA: New Society.

35. Zander, A. (1993). *Making boards effective: The dynamics of nonprofit governing boards.* San Francisco: Jossey-Bass.

36. Bolman & Deal. (1991).

37. Astin & Leland. (1991).
38. MacNeil. (2000).
39. Chrislip, D., & Larson, C. (1994). *Collaborative leadership: How citizens and civic leaders can make a difference.* San Francisco: Jossey-Bass. O'Connell. (1994). Rost. (1991). Torp, K., & Carlson, L. (1993). The new meaning of leadership for grassroots organizations. In R. Clifton & A. Dahms (Eds.), *Grassroots organizations.* Prospect Heights, IL: Waveland Press.
40. Rost. (1991).
41. Ibid., p. 181.
42. Torp & Carlson. (1993).
43. Zeldin & Camino. (1999).
44. Benson. (1997). Kretzmann & McKnight. (1993). MacNeil & Krensky. (1996). Olson et al. (2004).
45. Independent Sector. (2002). Smith. (1997).
46. Lakes. (1996). Olson et al. (2004).

CAROLE A. MACNEIL *is statewide director of the University of California's 4-H Youth Development Program, and national director of the 4-H Youth in Governance Initiative.*

The youth development movement represents a broad trend toward promoting opportunity and resilience over preventing delinquency and failure. While the topic of youth leadership is clearly relevant to this movement, the connection between the two topics remains for the most part unexplored and undefined. With this chapter we examine the ways that youth leadership connects to the much broader context of the youth development movement.

3

Youth leadership and youth development: Connections and questions

Cathann A. Kress

WEBSTER'S COLLEGIATE DICTIONARY defines a leader as "one who has commanding authority or influence; one able to direct the operations, activity, or performance," and states that the role of leader provides "a margin of advantage or superiority." The dictionary is a good place to begin, because leadership is a quality that few people can define. While many of us can name leaders, both good and bad, we may be hard-pressed to describe what good leaders have in common with each other. That is not unlike youth development, which most people struggle to define but can easily give an example of a program or organization they support, even if they cannot tell you what good programs have in common.

Ambiguous concepts

Both these concepts are laden with values about essential components, about who possesses "expert" knowledge and where to get accurate information related to basic ideas. This characterization is further complicated by other ambiguous concepts often confused with youth development and leadership, such as citizenship and character development. If we analyze leader development, we will find there is general agreement that successful leaders are defined by knowledge, competency, and character. If we parse those terms even finer, we focus on the tools of leadership, such as reflexive learning, communication, decision making, self-discipline, and other skills that, when combined, make effective action possible. It seems implicit in the term "leader" that abilities that aid in engaging others—motivating, managing conflict, and so forth—would be requirements as well. Few would disagree that leaders also require "character capacity," or an understanding of the difference between right and wrong, and the courage to do what is right.

It is easy to become convinced that, whether we are developing leaders or developing youth, intentions and actions should be the same because both have many overlapping aims and the differences may be revealed only when we focus at more than a superficial level. In the field of youth development, just as with youth leadership, it is generally understood that programs are designed to build a set of core competencies needed to participate successfully in adolescent and adult life. However, a notable and more important focus in youth development is to design programs to meet the developmental needs of youth.

What do we mean by youth development?

With youth, it is easy to pay direct attention to the changes that can be seen; in other words, their growth. It is easy to recognize these changes, such as spurts in height or weight, and the accompanying needs, such as longer pants or bigger shoes. While growth is a critical issue, in youth development we try to understand and pay attention to the needs that accompany *development*. What is the difference?

Quantity or quality?

Think of picking two apples. Both have grown equally, so their weights and circumferences (quantities) are the same. These two apples have similar growth but they taste and look very different. One apple is pale green, the other is a rosy red. The red apple did not grow more than the green apple; it simply ripened. This ripening, or maturation, is what development is all about. With youth development, the concern is with that which changes the *quality* of something—be it a muscle, a cognition, or an emotion.

We can measure and document growth easily; we have all stood on the scales or had our height marked on a door frame. These tangible indicators allow us to document factors that lead to and impede growth, but with development it is much more difficult. In the same way that we may not realize the importance a bee has in producing a ripe apple, we may miss the importance of contributors to the development of our youth. All youth will seek to develop fully, just as all apples would fully ripen given the right conditions. Whether we support them or not, youth will seek to meet their developmental needs, build skill sets and values, and use their skills, talents, energies, and time in self-gratifying and self-empowering ways.[1] It is easy to think that, without adult aid, young people would not be able to meet their own needs or develop skills and values, but the truth is that even very young children will create a framework of values and develop skills to manage daily life with or without adult aid. The question is: What kind of values and skills? Are the values and skills ultimately self-destructive or helpful in the life of that youth? Once we understand this part of human nature, we understand what motivates behavior and can begin to recognize unmet needs.

Focus on developmental needs

Youth development focuses on developmental needs and there is general recognition of two basic types: those that can be met and fulfilled, often referred to as *deficit* needs, and those that persist as a continuing driving force in our lives, the *being* needs.² To appreciate youth development completely, one must understand that higher needs, the being needs, matter only after all the basic needs have been met. In other words, the kinds of information and experiences that individuals seek at different points in their development will be determined by their unmet needs. Individuals for whom safety and belonging needs have not been met seek only experiences and information that will meet their basic needs for survival and connection. Information or experiences that are not directly connected to helping this individual meet his or her needs in a short time are irrelevant, no matter how attractive we might make them. For those whose unmet needs are at the being level, the focus is on experiences that create the opportunity to feel competent, powerful, and ultimately that their lives have meaning.

What makes the focus on developmental needs compelling is the understanding that if youth are not given positive outlets they may find potentially damaging alternatives. Youth may seek to belong through attention-seeking, promiscuous, or clinging behaviors. Youth with no productive opportunities for establishing their own competency can give up and avoid risk because it is easier not to try than to try and fail. And in a society where to be respected is to have power, winning respect through aggressive techniques is immensely important when there is so little power to be had.³

Some things cannot be taught

A rapidly changing society and a decreasing sense of community have reduced opportunities for many youth to receive the support necessary to become self-sufficient. Consequently, youth development focuses on the whole person within his or her context and not simply on one issue or problem or one set of skills. As a result, the outcomes of youth development are based on experiences and include complex dynamics, such as the development of character, citizenship, and leadership—things that cannot be taught didactically. This idea that some things cannot be taught but must be learned through experience is a key element of youth development. Development is supported through involvement with people or places that offer intellectual, spiritual, and emotional nurturing. The goal of youth development is to foster the maturity of individuals through experiences with people and activities that are both challenging and supportive.

The vision for youth development

Much of what we think of as youth development began with the vision of learning espoused by John Dewey. For Dewey, it was vitally important that education be not just the teaching of facts but the full integration of the skills and knowledge that youth have learned into their lives as citizens and human beings.[4] Dewey saw learning as a result of the interaction between youth and their environment, which meant that the experience was different for each individual, as it combined the new learning with previous learning and capacity.

Psychologist Lev Vygotsky emphasized not only the interactional nature of learning but also the importance of relationships with others for learning to be most effective.[5] What makes Vygotsky's theory relevant to youth development is the idea that instruction is most efficient when there are others who can assist in determining the correct balance of challenge and support. These others organize support to help learners complete a task near the upper end of their ability, or in the "zone of proximal development," as Vygotsky called it. In addition, they must then systematically withdraw this support as the learner moves to higher levels of ability.

A third major idea at the core of youth development is Bandura's social learning theory, which emphasizes the importance of observing and modeling the behaviors and attitudes of others.[6] Instruction works best by modeling desired behaviors of value to learners and by providing situations that allow learners to use or practice that behavior to improve retention.

These are basic ideas of youth development: some things cannot be taught but must be learned through experience, experiences are transformed by the individuals who participate in them, development occurs when a person is at a level that she or he can only achieve with help from another person, and we can learn from observing others and their actions. By putting these ideas into practice, youth development creates opportunities for youth to meet their developmental needs in productive ways. As a result, youth development approaches consider the *whole* young person as a central actor in his or her own development. With its focus on environments and opportunities, youth development is dependent on others as it occurs in the context of the family, community, and society. Finally, youth development is designed to focus on the positive outcomes we desire for all young people, such as becoming economically self-sufficient, remaining mentally and physically healthy, developing caring and cooperative relationships, and becoming a responsible member of and contributor to the community.

Leadership: One potential outcome

Just about every day, a youth walks into an organization and experiences a curriculum that has the intention of cultivating them as leaders. Whether or not that is the actual outcome is a discussion for later. While no one has suggested turning over the entire effort of the youth development field to the purpose of developing leaders, the distinction between the two endeavors is often blurred, which, coupled with the values of our culture, can create a pattern of efforts that favor young leaders and programs that focus on developing youth leaders and not primarily on developing youth. Is there anything wrong with that?

Opportunities for youth to experience independence and autonomy and to extend their influence are important elements of youth development, but they are not the primary elements, just as leadership is one potential outcome of youth development but not the only potential outcome. By confusing leadership and youth development, we force youth leadership programs to reside within the egalitarian mandate of the broader youth development field. This forces youth leadership to be seen through a lens that insists that nearly everyone can be a leader and that leadership abilities are distributed equally among various talent areas. This assumption contributes to leadership programs being watered down to the point that we have difficulty defining what leadership is and what these programs should offer. It also denies that some youth truly have the skills, talent, and character to be *exceptional* leaders.

Many people will argue that all youth *do* have the potential to be leaders, and one of the great myths of our society is that anyone who wields any influence is already a leader. While influence is one of the important constructs of effective leadership, it hardly contains the sum of leadership, no matter how much we might wish it. Leadership requires influence but it also requires substantial vision and some level of authority, whether formal or informal. Without any authority, there is no recognition from those who might be followers, and without that there is no leadership. However, the illusion that any and all teenagers could be leaders seems like a good thing to people who are uncomfortable with the reality that abilities are not equally distributed and that illusion is what generates a willingness to fund those programs eager to respond to it.

Issues in youth leadership

Youth leadership is the involvement of youth in responsible, challenging action that meets genuine needs, with opportunities for planning and decision making. For the most part, our culture places youth in powerless situations with no meaningful role other than as consumers. In addition, many adults do not understand that their role is not to mold participants in their programs but to provide tools and opportunities for youth to discover their unique spirit, genius, and public life.[7] This type of practice has not been modeled effectively, nor is it often valued. Well-intentioned adults often play the expert and re-create the power relations that keep youth in the role of consumer. If an adult is oriented toward serving as an expert, rather than facilitating the construction of knowledge, it does not seem likely that they will work effectively in partnership with youth.

Furthermore, there is often a disconnect between efforts at youth leadership education and the needs of today's youth. Too frequently, didactic methods are employed to teach an assortment of skills related to leadership in isolation from an experience of real influence or without being cast within issues related to authentic youth concerns. The idea of leadership as a developmental, lifelong trait that transcends day-to-day achievements has been replaced with a set of abilities. When this happens, we relegate leadership to a position of commodity to be displayed rather than as the unique state of mind and being it really is. It is true that the skills can be taught, but the accumulation of skills does not necessarily equal leadership. Leadership consists of skills, experiences, needs, and motivations and is a long and cumulative effort, not the single act of one individual who may serve as a catalyst for action. Although leadership typically resides in an individual, it is an effort far greater than the individual who fills the role. The cultivation of effective leadership requires the "calculated epiphany" that can occur through experiences that create the balance of challenge and support necessary to sustain influence.

When programs do generate leadership experiences to complement skill building, it is often hard to find the balance between actively engaging youth at their experience level and overwhelming them with too much responsibility. This difficult balance, what Vygotsky would have called an incorrect assessment of the zone of proximal development for youth leaders, can result in either youth with artificial status and no real power or youth burdened by responsibility that has no context within their former experience. As youth leaders struggle with these issues, reliance on adults can result in a lessened commitment and accountability from youth or the imposition of agendas from the adults. Finding that balance is more difficult than most experts in youth development initially imagined and embroils us in debates over what we are fostering—youth empowerment or youth partnership with adults. Youth empowerment suggests handing both the power and responsibility completely to youth, who are often unprepared for its reality. This autonomy is often nothing more than abandonment by adults who are unsure how to partner effectively with young leaders.

This becomes even more complicated when we consider the short leadership cycles in most youth groups, with the result being a loss of organizational capital (goal momentum and institutional memory). The continuous change in leadership, often on an annual basis, leads to a duplication of past projects and problems without the advantage of experience. Without the advantage of experience (which clearly benefits leadership), a strong new leader, armed with the skills of leadership and emerging talents, can easily succumb to the tendency to allow everything to be handled and executed by a small number of people. Not only is this discouraging to the group members (the other youth one hopes to lead), but it can also lead to a vacuum at the top when the leadership changes. The end result is a weakening of the capacity of youth leadership to sustain itself.

Our failure to conceptualize youth leaders outside an adult model of leadership is further evident in our selection processes for youth leaders. Do youth leaders represent their constituencies or the adults who empower them? "High-achieving," middle-class youth are often overrepresented among youth leaders, even in the leadership of groups intended to focus on at-risk youth. Often, successful youth organizations are elite driven, as they attract into leadership involved and achieving youth, who typically come from the more educated and included groups and reflect only a small segment of the total youth population. Should we not be worried about the gap between the youth affected by decisions being made and the youth making those decisions?

Of course, the issue of who gets to lead illustrates the broader challenges in developing or expanding effective programs for youth. Here, a different elitism, not tied to talent or ability but to who has access, has emerged. To have the opportunity of youth leadership, one must first participate, and the reality is that programs must be attractive and relevant to target audiences. In addition, income, race, and gender influence who participates, and youth from low-income communities—rural or urban—are least likely to be offered consistent support or a wide array of opportunities.[8]

54   YOUTH LEADERSHIP

It is far too easy to limit the power of youth by casting them solely as the "leaders of tomorrow." This rhetoric of the future means they can be excluded from the leadership of today. There is comfort for adults in perceiving youth only as leaders in incubation, particularly when we are unsure of the optimal balance of power and support. One of the great barriers to cultivating leadership among youth is the treatment of them solely as the "next generation." As a result, youth often fail to see themselves as actors in decision-making processes today.

Understanding youth leadership

As we define what youth leadership really is, it is instructive to view it as one potential outcome of youth development—an outcome that shares overlapping goals, values, and ideas with youth citizenship and character development—but that does not make leadership and development the same concept. It is heartening to understand that youth development can strengthen all three qualities shared with youth leadership, but that should not convince us to use the terms interchangeably, apply efforts toward each universally, or believe that one type of experience will affect them all equally. And while leadership is as fraught with our values and esteem as is character development, there is a difference between those outcomes we hope to build for *all* youth, such as character and citizenship, and those we recognize as being unique to individual youth, such as scientific inquisitiveness, musical talent, or exceptional leadership.

Just understanding youth leadership in these terms helps us to tie the concepts of best practices to the central ideas of quality youth development. To be effective, youth leadership efforts must focus on creating environments in which youth matter and are part of a supportive group that knows them well enough to recognize the optimal zone where they can achieve more only with help from other people—environments where youth skill development is encouraged through hands-on participation and by recognizing that experiences are transformed by the youth who participate in them. These environments must also involve caring adults who willingly allow youth to learn from observing their actions and who engage in actions worthy of being emulated. Leadership is one potential outcome of youth development, and positive developmental opportunities can help aspiring leaders to gain the experience that will propel them toward becoming exceptional leaders, just as historically we recognized the importance of apprenticeships in the preparation of journeymen and masters.

First, this understanding suggests that we must conceptualize youth leaders in different ways than we conceptualize adult leaders. Our inability to do so dooms youth leaders to failure for a couple of reasons: the more dependent role youth have in our culture—primarily as consumers of programs, ideas, and knowledge—and the short span of time most youth possess their leadership roles. Forcing youth to lead within traditional ideas of adult leadership tied to experience, authority, and adult concerns has the potential to create self-fulfilling prophecies for those who doubt youth's ability to lead. In addition, addressing this concern through attempts to strengthen youth power rather than through participation creates an artificial dynamic that often highlights the weaknesses of youth leaders rather than their strengths.

Second, identification of leadership potential among youth is another step toward meeting the needs of young leaders in productive ways. Many who work in the youth development field already recognize youth who naturally gravitate toward leadership roles, but little work has gone into tools to assess both capacity and achievement that would allow us to nurture leadership traits most effectively. This type of assessment could help to clarify the types of experiences a youth is ready for and the support still needed.

Finally, more research is needed to understand the different types of youth participation and how these ideas relate to and foster youth leadership by pursuing developmentally appropriate strategies for involving youth with adults in significant leadership.

Notes

1. Brendtro, L., Brokenleg, M., & Van Bockern, S. (1990). *Reclaiming youth at risk: Our hope for the future.* Bloomington, IN: National Education Service.
2. Maslow, A., & Lowery, R. (Eds.). (1998). *Toward a psychology of being* (3rd ed.). New York: Wiley & Sons.
3. Brendtro, Brokenleg, & Van Bockern. (1990).
4. Dewey, J. (1938). *Experience and education.* New York: Collier.
5. Vygotsky, L. S. (1978). Mind in society: The development of higher educational processes. In M. Cole, V. John-Steiner, S. Scribner, & E. Souberman (Eds.). Cambridge, MA: Harvard University Press.
6. Kearsley, G. (1994). *Social learning theory (A. Bandura).* Available on-line at http://www.gwu.edu/~tip/bandura.html [accessed December 1, 1999].
7. Boyte, H. C. (1999). Off the playground of civil society. *The Good Society, 9*(2), 1, 4–7.
8. David and Lucille Packard Foundation. (1999). *Future of children: When school is out, 9*(2).

CATHANN A. KRESS *is director of youth development for National 4-H Headquarters at the United States Department of Agriculture.*

The author of this chapter draws on adult leadership literature by presenting the adaptive leadership model. He then presents case studies of three existing youth leadership education programs, viewed through the lens of the adaptive leadership model. The analysis explores the conceptions of leadership that inform each program, the pedagogies employed by each program to teach leadership, and the alignment that exists between theory and practice. The study concludes with a grounded theory exploration of the theories and pedagogies employed in youth leadership education in the field today.

4

Exploring youth leadership in theory and practice

Max Klau

IN RECENT YEARS, a major shift in thinking has occurred among psychologists, educators, youth workers, and policymakers interested in adolescent development. The old focus on pathology, delinquency, and problem prevention has begun to be supplemented by a new interest in health, resilience, and opportunity development.[1] In an extensive review of the youth development literature, the Cornerstone Consulting Group notes that while the earlier focus resulted in a wealth of research exploring risk factors contributing to psychopathology, the new interest has begun to generate findings regarding protective factors that promote resiliency.[2] A partial list of these factors includes a supportive family life, social supports at school, religious values, aspirations, perceived self-competence, motivation to do well, supportive peers, a sense of agency, and initiative.[3]

Despite the growing academic interest in the topic, however, there is much about positive development that we still do not know. As Larson states: "We have a burgeoning field of developmental psychopathology but have a more diffuse body of research on the pathways whereby children and adolescents become motivated, directed, socially competent, compassionate, and psychologically vigorous adults. Corresponding to that, we have numerous research-based programs for youth aimed at curbing drug use, violence, suicide, teen pregnancy, and other problem behaviors, but lack a rigorous applied psychology of how to promote positive youth development."[4]

It is my belief that the notion of youth leadership education contains elements of theory and practice directly relevant to this emerging interest in promoting positive psychological development. Therefore, this pilot study aims to address this gap in the literature through an exploration of youth leadership education as it occurs in the field. Specifically, I intend to present case studies of three youth leadership education programs that address the following original research questions: *What conceptions of leadership inform the work of youth leadership educators in the field today? What pedagogical techniques are employed by programs to teach the model of leadership they espouse?* In addition, as I progressed through the research process, an additional question emerged: *From the perspective of the "adaptive leadership" model presented in this chapter, how might we diagnose the relationship between theory and practice encountered at these programs?*

Background

Naturally, any analysis of youth leadership should avail itself of the considerable body of academic literature devoted to leadership in general. However, it is important to recognize that scholars have highlighted the field's problematic lack of clarity and coherence regarding a definition of leadership.[5]

Rost offers the most relevant critique. In his book *Leadership for the Twenty-First Century*, he states: "The word *leadership* (and, to some extent, related words such as *lead, leader,* and *leading*) are used in scholarly and popular publications, organizational newsletters and reports, and the media to mean very different things that have little to do with any considered notion of what leadership actually is. . . . In 1990, leadership is a word that has come to mean all things to all people."[6]

Rost's critique appears to hold true for the work related to youth leadership as well. Consider, for example, the following passage from a book devoted to an academic exploration of youth leadership. Van Linden and Fertman introduce the notion of leadership by claiming: "Adolescents are busy leading in many ways—maybe not as presidents of their class or members of student government, but in more subtle ways. They are baby-sitting, working a job, and volunteering. They are spending time with peers, hanging out at the mall, and being involved in school or community."[7]

In their effort to assert that "all teenagers have the potential to lead," Van Linden and Fertman appear to suggest that engaging in almost any activity can qualify as leadership.[8]

Additional readings further complicate the issue. According to various sources, engaging in youth leadership involves facilitating ice-breakers and group cooperation games,[9] religious outreach and proselytizing skills,[10] working on active listening skills, and developing abilities like courage, commitment, and humor.[11] Apparently, the concept of youth leadership is broad enough to include both brief, nondisclosive, group-building games as well as ongoing religious outreach based on disclosure of a deeply held faith; youth leadership occurs through both active listening and through joining the school band; adolescents lead both through becoming class president and by hanging out at the mall. Ultimately, the multitude of activities presumed to fall under the domain of youth leadership lends support to Rost's critique.

If youth leadership can be almost anything, then what exactly is it?

In light of this confusion, it is perhaps not surprising to hear the results of a ten-year Carnegie Foundation study that examined 120 youth-based organizations located across the United States. The research found a profound disconnect between current efforts at youth leadership education and the experiences and needs of today's kids. Findings suggest that many programs "often depend, at best, on implicit unexamined ideas about how young people develop leadership traits and what being a leader entails. At worst, youth leadership programs are described as an almost negative space into which practitioners project their own beliefs about what youth need."[12]

In search of clarity: The Heifetz framework

It is my belief that Ronald Heifetz's model of "adaptive leadership" holds particular value for academics and practitioners interested in working with youth. The Heifetz framework presents theoretical distinctions that bring considerable clarity to the question of what is meant by the term *leadership*. It also includes pedagogical tools that are directly relevant to the teaching of leadership. In addition, it was my encounter with this framework that inspired this research exploring how youth leadership education occurs in the field.

After reviewing the major movements in leadership theory (the trait approach, the situational approach, contingency theory, and the transactional approach), Heifetz highlights a conceptual problem that runs through much of this work: "These four general approaches attempt to define leadership objectively, without making value judgments. When defining leadership in terms of prominence, authority, and influence, however, these theories introduce value biases implicitly without declaring their introduction and without arguing for the necessity of the values introduced."[13]

While he recognizes that these approaches have provided some useful insights, Heifetz makes a strong case that this lack of clarity is problematic. He notes that leadership has been exercised in the past by figures such as Rosa Parks and Mohandas Gandhi, who made an impact from a societal position that initially lacked formal prominence, authority, or influence.

On the basis of this insight, Heifetz argues for making a distinction between authority and leadership. While the two concepts are related and frequently confused, one need not possess authority to exercise leadership. Authority involves holding a formal position, such as student council president, teacher, principal, or CEO. However, as the examples of Parks and Gandhi demonstrate, individuals without authority may still attempt to exercise leadership. Because young people rarely wield formal authority in society, this critique of the literature on adult leadership is particularly salient for scholars interested in exploring the practice of youth leadership.

Heifetz also distinguishes between *technical* and *adaptive* challenges. Technical challenges are relatively straightforward problems that we already know how to solve. Far more complex—and ultimately far more important—are adaptive challenges that have no clear solution and frequently require changes in the values and behaviors of the group. To put this distinction into more concrete form: planning a bus route in Montgomery, Alabama, was a technical challenge; transforming the relationship between blacks and whites in the Jim Crowe south was an adaptive challenge. Again, this notion is salient to the theory and practice of youth leadership; it allows us to differentiate between hanging out at the mall or playing in the school band and, for example, advocating against drunk driving.

In addition to providing these theoretical distinctions, Heifetz employs three key pedagogical tools in his leadership education methodology:[14]

- *Case-in-point learning.* By encouraging students to discuss the real-time dynamics of the class itself, students in Heifetz's class have a chance to explore who is being given informal authority, who is being marginalized, and how important dynamics like race or gender affect the group. The experience feels radically different from a traditional lecture or discussion, and results in a particularly personal and deep type of learning.

- *Below-the-neck learning.* Heifetz recognizes that the experience of exercising leadership is considerably more intense than the experience of simply talking about leadership. It requires courage and the ability to tolerate emotionally uncomfortable circumstances for long periods. By creating a safe space in which students can both experience and reflect on this discomfort, Heifetz demonstrates that it is valuable to engage the emotions as well as the intellect.
- *Reflective practice.* Students are constantly provided with opportunities to reflect on why they made particular choices or responded in particular ways. The result, once again, is a uniquely personal and deep educational experience.

Taken as a whole, the Heifetz framework includes elements of theory and practice that are directly relevant to the work of youth leadership education. His model is helpful in addressing the confusion that emerges from the literature on both youth and adult leadership, and provides useful tools for diagnosing the pedagogical practices in use in the field. For these reasons, his work both inspires and informs this research.

Nature of the research

The purpose of this research is to begin the process of bringing both attention and clarity to the topic of youth leadership. Specifically, my goal is to understand both the theory and practice of youth leadership and youth leadership education as it occurs in the field by exploring the following research questions: *What conceptions of leadership inform the work of youth leadership educators in the field today? What pedagogy is employed by programs to teach the model of leadership they espouse?* In addition, I examine: *How might we diagnose the relationship between theory and practice encountered at these programs from the perspective of the "adaptive leadership" model?*

In an effort to address these questions, I engage here in a grounded-theory exploration of adolescent youth leadership education.[15] Specifically, I present multiple case studies involving three existing adolescent-focused youth leadership programs.[16] Through these case studies, I seek both to understand each program in detail and to gain some more generalizable insights into the variety of theories and practices currently in use in the field. Naturally, my knowledge of the Heifetz framework has informed my interpretations of what I encountered in the field.

Data collection for the study involved site visits, direct observation, review of educational and promotional documents, informal interviews with participants, and formal interviews with educators and senior staff.[17] Programs were selected as cases for this study on the basis of the following criteria:

The program focused on an adolescent population.[18]
The program literature presented an explicit focus on the concept of leadership.
The program included a pedagogy designed to teach leadership, as opposed to being simply a social club or organizational committee.
The program explicitly promoted the importance of civic engagement in the sense of communal and political responsibility; it went beyond the limited scope of promoting mastery of a particular domain such as sports or the arts.
The program had a reputation in the field for quality programming and strong impact. I endeavored to visit programs that have received positive recommendations from youth development professionals in the field.
By necessity, programs were selected on the basis of convenience, that is, in terms of whether both location and timing were manageable given my status as a full-time student.

Two clarifications must be made regarding the cases selected. First, it must be understood that these three case studies are in no way a representative sample of the general population of youth leadership programs. Second, this research is not intended to present a formal evaluation of the programs selected. Such an evaluation would require alternate methodology and a different level and type of commitment from the programs studied.

Rather, the goal is to begin developing a theoretical framework for understanding and diagnosing the practice of youth leadership as it occurs in the field. For this reason, the names of all programs and individuals encountered in the field have been altered in an attempt to maintain their confidentiality. Because the conversations and pedagogies I encountered represent the heart of my research questions, I have made every effort to present those details in as faithful and accurate a manner as possible.

Data analysis included both single-case and cross-case analysis.[19] The validity of the interpretations I present in my analysis was tested through member checks[20] and by working with an interpretive community.[21] A series of codes related to leadership conceptions and pedagogical techniques emerged from this process and were used in rigorous analysis of transcript data and observation notes.

In the report that follows, I present a brief case study of each program I visited. I include an overview and background for each program, and then present data relevant to my research questions. Following each case study I briefly analyze the theory and practice I encountered at each program on the basis of the elements of the Heifetz framework presented earlier. After the final case study, I conclude with a cross-case analysis of all three cases. In this section, I summarize my major findings and offer suggestions for future research.

National leadership conference case study

Background and overview of program

The National Leadership Conference (NLC) is a national organization that has been in existence for more than forty years. According to its literature, the NLC's mission statement is "to seek, recognize, and develop leadership potential commencing with high school sophomores." Every year the organization runs programs in all fifty states; one representative from every high school in the state is invited to attend a residential seminar.

I observed a four-day program held at a hotel in a small New England city. At the seminar I attended, more than 90 percent of high schools in the state—both public and private—were represented. The nearly two hundred students in attendance represented a remarkable cross section of the state's social and economic diversity. Representatives from the poorest inner-city schools sat next to peers from some of the nation's most elite private institutions.

Participants appeared to be selected for the program through a variety of processes. Some students I talked to told me they had to compete in an essay-writing contest in which they composed an answer to the question "What is leadership?" They were there because they wrote the winning essay. Others told me there was no competition at their school; they were simply invited by a teacher because they were the president of the sophomore class or of the student council. Still others said they were invited by a teacher or guidance counselor even though they were not in a position of formal authority in their school. Eventually my conversation with the director, Sarah, confirmed that students were there as the result of a variety of processes. While the program encouraged essay contests to determine representatives, there were no firm criteria by which schools selected individuals to attend the conference.

Once there, however, it was clear that the program sought to treat each participant as exceptional. Over the course of my time at the program, the director, the many facilitators I spoke with—even the program nurse—spoke in glowing terms of the intelligence, creativity, and idealism of the students they encountered there.

Conception of leadership informing the program

It is difficult to identify a clear conception of leadership at the NLC. When I asked the director to explain to me the NLC's conception of leadership, she recited the organization's mission statement: "to seek, recognize, and develop leadership potential starting with high school sophomores." When I asked what the

NLC means by "developing leadership potential," the director mentioned two slogans I would hear frequently over the remaining three days of the program: "We teach them how to think, not what to think," she explained. "And we encourage them to respectfully challenge the viewpoints that they hear." Both of these phrases are echoed in the NLC literature and Web site. However, she continued, saying,

Something we look for is not just the person who is doing everything all the time. It's the person who shares ideas and draws out ideas from other people who aren't so willing to share. . . . A lot of times groups "choose" leaders. Sometimes it's just the prettiest or most outgoing; that's not really what we look for though. Our evaluators go more by experience. They have all been around for a couple years and know what to look for. . . . We don't write down leadership qualities because it is hard to put into words. We don't want to tell them what a leader is. We are not all the same. We don't teach them what a leader is; we give them a chance to do it.

After speaking with the director, however, I interviewed a staff member I noticed making rounds throughout the room. He told me he is part of a selection committee responsible for choosing which participants would be selected to continue on to the national conference later in the year. Over the course of the four-day program, a team of evaluators would select a boy and a girl who would represent their state at the NLC World Conference, to be held several months later. None of the kids knew they were being evaluated in this way; the staff member explained that telling the participants beforehand might bias their behavior. At the final ceremony on the last day of the program, the names of the selected participants (as well as two alternates) would be announced.

I asked him whether NLC has a formally stated conception of leadership and he shook his head. "I am not sure," he said. I asked what he was looking for, and he said, "I am looking to see whether other kids seem to follow along; I look for the kid who is creative and gets things done."

Later on, I spoke to another member of the evaluation team. She also was unaware of any formally stated conceptions of leadership that the program endorsed. When I asked what she was looking for as an evaluator, she said, "I think it is about really listening to each other. Still holding on to your own ideas, but really listening, and then taking that back to the schools."

The difference between the answers of these two evaluation team members surprised me; they seemed to be looking for two dramatically different participants. In addition, I found it hard to understand the connection between the director's statements regarding the NLC's conception of leadership and the remarks by the selection committee.

Pedagogical techniques employed by the NLC

The NLC pedagogy is based on clear guidelines from the national office. Local programs are to present a series of seven panels, exploring topics that can be chosen by the local staff. At the conference I attended, topics included the importance of voting, a mock trial, genetic testing, the media, "rights of young adults," education, and volunteerism. Each panel included adults who are experts in the field. For example, the mock trial was run by a real state judge, and the panel on media included local reporters and media executives.

Following each panel was "family time," an activity that allowed each student to interact with the panel members in a slightly more intimate format. The students split into four groups and headed to each corner of the room. Then, each panelist spent five minutes fielding questions at each station before rotating on to the next corner. The time with each panelist was brief, but clearly gave the participants more access and insight than would be possible in the large-group setting. When each panelist's five minutes were up, the students in that corner all yelled "*Outstanding!*"

It was immediately apparent that the NLC puts a great deal of emphasis on this sort of enthusiastic cheering. Time between panels was filled with an incredible amount of energy as tables of students "challenged" each other with cheers ("We got the spirit, yes we do! We got the spirit, how about you?!"), or individuals stood up to try to get the whole group to sing songs such as "Buttercup" or "Lean on Me."

While this enthusiasm and energy was initially inspiring, by the third and fourth day of the program I found myself exhausted by the endless cycle of panels and cheering. As the program progressed, I was surprised to find that members of the evaluation committee removed students from the list of finalists if they stopped cheering or appeared to express frustration with the constant high levels of enthusiasm. In this sense, the cheering (which I had assumed to be a peripheral part of the NLC experience) actually played a central role in the program's pedagogy.

By the final day of the program, I realized that many participants shared my own confusion regarding the importance of the constant cheering. When I asked participants what they had learned about leadership, many responded that they were not sure what all the cheering had to do with leadership. Others stated that they felt they had not had a second to think because of the constant noise. Still others argued that enthusiasm must be an important part of leadership and seemed to enjoy the constant spirit and energy.

The program ended with all participants and staff gathered for a final ceremony in the main hall. To wild cheers and applause, the director announced the male and female selected as winners by the evaluation committee. I had noticed these students during my time at the program; they are both outgoing, attractive, popular, funny, polite, self-assured, and friendly: the kind of students that everybody in high school likes. After four days of panels, questions, and cheering, the program publicly anointed these individuals as the "best" leaders—the ones who have what it takes to represent the state at the world conference.

The selection left me feeling bewildered about all I had witnessed over the four days at the program. The enthusiasm and genuine goodwill of everyone on staff was obvious and undeniable. There was also no doubt that, on the one hand, the program pedagogy promotes civic involvement, community service, the importance of intellectual engagement with current events, and the validity of questioning authority. On the other hand, the constant cheering seemed to be the real pedagogical focus, a fact that undermines or contradicts much of the espoused values of the program.

Despite the idealistic rhetoric, the entire evaluation process publicly rewarded those extroverted participants with the stamina to maintain the appearance of unquestioning hyper-enthusiasm for the experience for four days straight. As I left the hotel, I couldn't help but recall the sentiment of the Carnegie Foundation study presented in the introduction of this paper: "[Youth leadership] programs often depend, at best, on implicit unexamined ideas about how young people develop leadership traits and what being a leader entails. At worst, youth leadership programs are described as an almost negative space into which practitioners project their own beliefs about what youth need."[22]

An adaptive leadership perspective on the National Leadership Conference

The most striking aspect of this program is its lack of clarity regarding what it means by leadership. The mission statement ("to seek, recognize, and develop leadership potential starting with high school sophomores") puts leadership at the heart of the program's vision, but does not present any notion of what is meant by the term. The NLC's literature highlights the values of civic engagement, community service, and critical thinking, and in many ways the pedagogy supports these values. However, for obvious reasons, the absence of a clearly espoused conception of leadership in a program that allegedly teaches youth leadership is problematic.

When viewed through the lens of the Heifetz framework, some distinctions emerge that clarify the assumptions informing the work done by the NLC.

Leadership versus authority. The NLC appears to place a very strong emphasis on the importance of authority. The core of the program's pedagogy involves a series of seven expert panels in which the adolescent participants listen to lectures or talks given by adult authorities. While the panels focus on subjects that promote civic engagement (such as law, medicine, journalism, and community service), the pedagogy suggests that for the most part students can exercise leadership only by attaining an adult position of authority.

In addition, although the program endorses "respectful questioning of authority," by placing so clear an emphasis on constant cheering, the pedagogy seems to demand unquestioning enthusiasm for authority. This disconnect between theory and practice at the program challenges the effectiveness of the NLC at its core. The pedagogy appears to undermine one of the few explicit values presented in the NLC's amorphous conception of leadership.

Technical versus adaptive challenges. In the absence of a clear conception of leadership, it is difficult to diagnose whether the NLC is focused on addressing technical or adaptive challenges. It is telling, however, that the program deliberately avoids controversial subjects and places such strong emphasis on cheering. It appears as though the clearest message to many of the students is that leadership involves constant upbeat enthusiasm. According to the Heifetz model, this educational message is a problem, as addressing adaptive challenges is sure to create some amount of discomfort. Teaching young people to remain constantly enthusiastic may encourage them to avoid addressing difficult but important issues.

Case-in-point learning. The NLC pedagogy is almost completely focused on frontal lectures and panels interspersed with brief question-and-answer sessions. I observed no instances in which students were given the opportunity to reflect on their own experiences or learn from the group dynamics.

Below-the-neck learning. Again, the core of the NLC pedagogy was frontal lectures and panels. Aside from the enjoyment and group coherence (or at least the appearance of these emotions) elicited by the ubiquitous cheering, very little emphasis was placed on engaging participants emotionally. As many of the students eventually began to wonder, it is reasonable to question why teaching leadership demands mandating a state of perpetual enthusiasm.

Reflective practice. The students had no formal opportunities to stop and reflect on their own actions. There were some spaces, such as family time, for students to ask questions of others, but never of themselves. On the contrary, questioning the experience in any way was discouraged by the program; students who stopped cheering were taken out of the running to move on to the world conference.

In conclusion, it is problematic that this program is so amorphous in theory and inconsistent in practice. However, despite these considerable criticisms, it should be made clear that the intentions of everyone involved in this program were completely commendable. My sense was that many of the staff members were frustrated by their own lack of clarity regarding the purpose of the program but had few opportunities themselves to reflect on their work or engage with relevant literature.

The NLC may be an example of the sort of uninformed and confused practice that previous studies have highlighted as being all too common in the field of youth leadership education. Ultimately, however, it is promising to consider how this national program affecting thousands of youth annually might be improved through exposure to relevant research and best practices.

Jewish Leadership Organization case study

Overview and background of the program

The Jewish Leadership Organization (JLO) is devoted to teaching Jewish young people about the connection between Jewish values and civic engagement. I observed a four-day conference at a hotel in Washington, D.C., but this was actually just one component of a year-long Jewish leadership curriculum. Groups of participants came from a variety of communities (Boston, Dallas, Phoenix, and New Haven). All thirty-three students were involved in a particular Jewish day school or supplementary religious school in their home community, and at this point (late January) they had all already spent a semester exploring the connection between Jewish values and civic engagement using a classroom-based curriculum developed by JLO.

There really was no selection process by which participants arrived at this conference. They were all students who chose to take this class and were able to pay the several hundred dollars required to participate in this field trip component of the course. Following these intense four days in the nation's capital, students were expected to return home to organize and execute their own community service project.

Conception of leadership informing the program

On the first night of the program, JLO founder and executive director Rabbi Marc Stein delivered a keynote address. On our schedule, the topic of the speech was presented as "Jews as agents for positive social change."

Marc began with a question about leadership: "How many people have been in a position of leadership?" Many students raised their hands. Then he asked, "How many can think of a time when they exercised leadership?" A few hands tentatively went up. "They are two different things," he explained.

> One involves being elected. The other is something you can do every day. Let me give you an example. You are at a meeting and someone is clearly left out. If you go over and talk to that person, that is an act of leadership. Jewish leadership requires seeing the world in that way—who can we reach out to for help? I call it "spiritual heroism." Let me give you an important saying: "In a place where there is no one of moral courage, try to be such a person." ... Out of the very core of our tradition comes a demand, a requirement, a challenge to exercise our leadership to help those in need. So how do you convey from generation to generation a tradition that conveys the values you see on the walls? Open your eyes guys! Compassion, justice, love all of God's creations! That is what we are here to explore in the next four days!

It was an inspiring moment. Marc's passion for these ideals is unmistakably real, as is his commitment to the task. The keynote address also made it abundantly clear what the JLO means when it speaks of leadership. In the minds of everyone in the audience, these words would frame and inform every subsequent moment of the program.

Pedagogical techniques employed by the JLO

Over the course of the four-day program, the JLO employed a wide variety of pedagogies. Students listened to a lecture by a renowned retired executive from a major Jewish organization, and they asked questions of expert panels addressing issues such as AIDS and affirmative action. They took field trips to visit advocacy organizations working on issues such as homelessness and hunger, and engaged in an afternoon of community service at a variety of locations around the city. They spent an afternoon involved in "Street Torah," an activity in which students handed out food and clothing to the homeless in a local park, and were given time to engage these destitute men and women in an extended conversation. Considerable time was devoted to small group discussion and debate, and each outing was followed by an opportunity for collective reflection on the experience. The program concluded with each group visiting one of their congressional representatives on Capitol Hill. According to participant feedback, this wide array of pedagogical techniques employed by the program provided an engaging and provocative educational experience.

For the most part, the connection between the very clear conception of leadership presented the first evening and all subsequent activities was immediately apparent. The one issue I encountered that seemed to detract from the effectiveness of the program involved some social dynamics that evolved over the course of the program. As frequently occurs, two or three awkward or outspoken participants were marginalized by the group. While these dynamics were hardly unusual or out of the ordinary, the program did not really address issues of ostracism or marginalization within the group. In this otherwise carefully conceived and executed program, the issue represented one area where the theory of "spiritual heroism" might be more directly connected to practice.

An adaptive leadership perspective on the Jewish Leadership Organization

In terms of its espoused conception of leadership, the JLO could not be more different from the NLC. The notion of "spiritual heroism" was quite clearly presented and informed much of the practice of the program. It was not surprising to find that, unlike at the NLC, students here did not seem confused about the purpose of the program or the relevance of various activities to exercising leadership.

Authority versus leadership. The JLO was actually explicit in presenting a similar distinction. The director made it clear that one need not hold a formal position to exercise leadership, and the program included a variety of pedagogies that were not focused on frontal lectures by adult authorities. Students worked in small groups, engaged in community service, and experienced Street Torah. The program presented opportunities for youth to experience leadership in a more personal and immediate way.

Technical versus adaptive challenges. Again, the JLO was explicit in promoting the importance of advocacy and working for social change. Students were encouraged to think about difficult challenges like homelessness, hunger, and AIDS in a sophisticated manner that allowed for uncomfortable emotions and discussions of controversial issues. Based on the notion of "spiritual heroism," students were encouraged to try to address these adaptive challenges.

Case-in-point learning. As the example of the marginalized students demonstrates, the program did not use the dynamics of the group as a focus for learning. On the one hand, the director was aware of the importance of these dynamics, but he suggested that there is only so much that can be done to manage the way chaperones address these issues. While there are no easy answers related to managing these social dynamics, this remains a frontier at which the JLO could work to bring the pedagogy even more in line with its espoused theory of leadership.

Below-the-neck learning. The variety of pedagogies employed by the program encourages below-the-neck learning in a number of ways. Activities like visiting with a congressional representative or interviewing a homeless person all challenged participants at an emotional level in a way that lectures and panels do not. In addition, the JLO allowed space for difficult emotions by allowing students to discuss issues like AIDS and homelessness with openness and candor.

Reflective practice. The JLO makes a deliberate and continuous effort to build reflection into its pedagogy. Following events like community service, Street Torah, and visiting advocacy organizations, participants were given an opportunity to explore their experiences and feelings together.

Overall, when viewed through the lens of the adaptive leadership model, this program avoids many of the problems highlighted in the youth leadership literature. The JLO is carefully conceived at the theoretical level and thoughtfully executed at the practice level. This clarity and deliberateness allows for a degree of alignment between theory and practice that, relative to other programs, ensures a more impactful and effective youth leadership education experience.

Institute for Justice and Leadership case study

Overview and background of program

The Institute for Justice and Leadership (IJL) is a national organization dedicated to combating racism, sexism, and bigotry. The program I visited brought together twenty-two high school sophomores and juniors at a scenic New England summer camp facility. I was told that this group was slightly smaller than the average in states with a more established program. Although the organization has been running its summer youth leadership program for many years in other states, this particular camp is less than five years old.

From what I can gather, students hear about the IJL summer experience through word of mouth and apply to attend. Participants I spoke to told me they heard about the program through a church group or through their parents or a teacher or guidance counselor. Although there is a brief application, my sense from the staff is that, because of the newness of the program, very few applications were denied this year. The result of this recruitment method was a relatively small, phenomenally diverse group of young people genuinely interested in and committed to the mission of the IJL.

Conception of leadership informing the program

When I asked Andrea, one of the program's codirectors, to explain the IJL's conception of leadership, she looked puzzled.

"That's hard to explain," she said. "Although I have been involved with the IJL for four years, I have only been in this codirector position for about three months. So I am not so up on this. I can definitely tell you our mission statement, though: We fight bias, bigotry, and racism through advocacy, conflict resolution, and education."

Lewis, the other codirector, had a similar response. Asked to explain the IJL's conception of leadership, he said, "Hmmm. We talk more about 'community relations' or 'race relations' here, I would say. What I would call the leader of the future is knowing your own biases, prejudices, and fears."

Once again, I am surprised to find that a program that bills itself as a leadership training experience has so little clarity on what the term means. It is obvious that the staff members I spoke with were intimately familiar with and deeply committed to the mission of combating bias, bigotry, and racism. Indeed, the pedagogy for the entire week was focused on raising awareness of these issues. However, the notion of what it means to be a leader on these issues, either at the camp or back home, seemed to receive very little thought.

Pedagogical techniques employed by the IJL

The IJL relies almost exclusively on group processing, case-in-point learning, and reflective practice. Over the course of the retreat there were no lectures or expert panels. All the time was devoted to open and honest discussions regarding race, religion, and gender. Through structured discussions and group activities, participants were encouraged to explore how these dynamics play out in the daily interactions within the group.

On the final day of the program, participants engaged in a "segregation exercise," in which participants were separated into small groups and told not to communicate outside of their group. Counselors encouraged this isolation while waiting for the participants to "break" the exercise, which they inevitably did. The experience concluded with a long processing session in which students explored the case-in-point dynamics that occurred and how they relate to wider issues of racism, bigotry, and bias.

The result of this constant focus on group dynamics appears to be a profound learning experience. Students engaged in a deep and personal way with some very painful and controversial issues in a safe and supportive environment. According to participant feedback, the cathartic experience of shared vulnerability and pain was ultimately a validating and empowering experience.

Although the experience was clearly powerful, the program spent very little time exploring what it means to act on this new awareness back home. Trying to be a leader in addressing issues of racism or bigotry outside the program's safe space can be dangerous, and the program treated the issue as something of an afterthought. My sense was that this oversight was the result of the program's amorphous conception of leadership. Although this is just one component of an otherwise carefully crafted program, in this case, greater clarity of theory would surely result in more effective practice.

An adaptive leadership perspective on the Institute for Justice and Leadership

The IJL differs from the other two programs in that the pedagogy focuses almost completely on case-in-point learning. For an entire week the participants explored their own religions, races, sexual orientations, and backgrounds, and had serious and open conversations about how these dynamics played out in the group. It is problematic, however, that the program was so unclear about what was meant by leadership. Being aware of these issues is not necessarily the same thing as being a leader trying to work on these issues outside of the IJL community. Once again, it seems likely that this lack of clarity regarding the notion of leadership served to undermine the impact of the program.

Authority versus leadership. Although the IJL does not explicitly make this distinction, everything about its pedagogy makes it clear that you need not have a position of formal authority to have an impact. In the absence of lectures and expert panels, the whole focus of the program was on relating to peers in a way that could hardly be more personal or relevant. However, since the IJL does not really know what it means by leadership, it misses an important opportunity. Exploring these issues in a safe environment at a summer camp is one thing; working on these issues at school with one's peers is quite another. By not examining the dangers of leadership or the ways groups will resist change, the IJL leaves its participants with minimal insight into how to take the experience home.

Technical versus adaptive challenges. More than any other program I visited, the IJL stayed focused on adaptive challenges. Every moment of the experience was characterized by difficult and emotionally sensitive conversations. The program did a remarkable job of trusting the participants to grapple with these challenges in a fashion that was so open and mature. Again, however, the program could be improved by including some analysis of the dangers and threats that result from working on adaptive challenges. Discussions that can be had during IJL may not be so easy to have back home, and the program could be improved by preparing participants to understand and address these challenges.

Case-in-point learning. The case-in-point model is at the core of the IJL's pedagogy. It is quite literally impossible to imagine participants being marginalized as occurred at the JLO. Dynamics of ostracism would be immediately explored; at the IJL program I visited, even the most unusual kids were considered an integral part of the group experience. The fact that this program has used this model for years is a powerful testament to the fact the young people can be trusted to engage these sensitive issues.

Below-the-neck learning. During my stay at this program I saw several people, including the codirector, on the edge of tears. Even as an experienced educator who was merely observing the event, I personally found the segregation exercise to be emotionally exhausting. The program is about as far from a sterile question-and-answer experience as can be imagined.

Reflective practice. The IJL doesn't so much make time for reflective practice; it is more accurate to say that the whole program is reflective practice. Nothing occurs without being examined and explored as a group. This clearly makes for some very deep and personal learning, especially when considered in relation to the other programs I visited.

Overall, the IJL comes closer than the other programs I visited to actually using the Heifetz model with young adults. That the program is national and has been operating for years is a powerful testament both to the program's ability to facilitate these discussions safely and to the capacity of young people to handle this emotionally challenging type of learning. It is intriguing to consider how effective this demanding program might be if it was based on a more carefully considered notion of what it means to teach when it claims to teach leadership.

Cross case analysis

While the three case studies presented here are not a generalizable sample of all existing youth leadership programs, they incorporate a diverse array of theories and practices related to youth leadership education. Surely they provide a window into understanding some general themes related to the work that is currently occurring in the field. In the section that follows, I consider all three programs in the light of the two research questions that informed this study: *What conceptions of leadership inform the work of youth leadership educators in the field today? What pedagogical techniques are employed by programs to teach the model of leadership they espouse?* In the context of exploring these questions, I also include my diagnosis of the connection between theory and practice at each program, informed by my knowledge of the "adaptive leadership" model.

Question 1: What conceptions of leadership inform the work of youth leadership educators in the field today?

The most important finding to emerge from this research is the fact that two of the three programs I visited had no clear conception of what they meant by leadership. Significantly, these were the two national programs, which touch hundreds, if not thousands, of young people annually. Also important is the fact that these programs pulled students out of their home communities for four to six days explicitly to teach them about leadership. It is remarkable that so much infrastructure, manpower, and effort goes into an educational endeavor that is so amorphous at its core.

In particular, the National Leadership Conference stands out as an example of the problems that arise when practice is based on unclear or unexamined assumptions of what is meant by leadership. Although the NLC lacks a carefully considered conception of leadership, its pedagogy presents some strong but implicit biases and values. The emphasis placed on adult authorities by lectures and panels, the focus on enthusiastic cheering, and the selection of "winners" who are the "best" leaders all imply an assumption that authority, prominence, and charismatic influence are essential to leadership.

My research suggests that, by subscribing to these largely unexplored assumptions about leadership, the program involves a pedagogy that in many ways undermines the central values the NLC claims to promote. While championing the notion of "respectful questioning of authority," the program mandates constant enthusiasm for all facets of the experience. While claiming to teach "how to think, not what to think," the program allows almost no space for reflection, and actively discourages questions about the program's purpose and pedagogy. Thus, in many ways, the lack of clarity at the NLC has consequences that appear to undermine the program's best intentions.

The other program lacking a clear definition of leadership was the Institute for Justice and Leadership. Compared to the NLC, however, the IJL demonstrated considerable alignment between theory and practice. Despite its amorphous conception of leadership, the program had a clear mission statement about ending bias, bigotry, and discrimination. The pedagogy of the program consistently focused on advancing this mission. Once again, however, the lack of clarity regarding leadership did appear to relate to educational limitations of the program. In this case, the result of an amorphous conception of leadership appears to be a missed opportunity to educate students on how to exercise leadership effectively on these issues when they return to their communities. By treating the issue of "taking it home" as an afterthought, the IJL may limit participants' abilities to act on their heightened awareness to issues of bias and bigotry when they return to their home communities.

The other program in the study presented a quite explicit conception of leadership. The Jewish Leadership Organization's notion of "spiritual heroism" was clearly stated in the first hours of the program. In addition, the pedagogies employed by this program were closely aligned with this espoused theory of leadership. On the basis of this research, it seems reasonable to assert that this clarity of purpose results in readily apparent educational benefits. For the most part, programs with clearly espoused theories of leadership incorporate pedagogies that effectively advance, as opposed to undermine, stated values.

It is important to recognize, however, that programs inevitably teach more than just their espoused conceptions of leadership. For example, the NLC never talked about the "great individual" conception of leadership, but much of the pedagogy reinforced this theoretical stance.

Thus, in an effort to answer my first research question more effectively, I engaged in a grounded theory analysis of the data to generate a list of conceptions of leadership that are embedded in the pedagogies I encountered. The result, presented in Table 4.1, represents a partial but, I hope, informative overview of notions of leadership currently employed, either explicitly or implicitly, in the field of youth leadership education today.

It is interesting to note the degree to which various programs incorporate a number of these conceptions. For example, the IJL lacks an espoused conception of leadership. Yet the pedagogy it employs clearly promotes several conceptions presented here. For example, it endorses notions of moral and spiritual leadership, relational leadership, and civic leadership. Practitioners in the field may find it helpful to review this list and evaluate which conceptions are implicit in the work they do. Making these conceptions explicit may facilitate greater alignment between theory and practice, potentially enhancing the quality of education that occurs at each program.

Finally, this research is based on a recognition that we know very little about effective positive development practices for youth. It should be made clear that many of these conceptions of leadership

Table 4.1. Leadership definitions in youth leadership education

Conception	Definition	Example
Civic leadership	Interest in and engagement with issues of broad public interest	All programs (required for inclusion in this study)
Charismatic leadership	Ability to influence peers through enthusiasm, extroversion, or creativity	Emphasis on cheering and extroversion at NLC
Leadership as formal authority	Attainment of a position of formal authority in a business or organization	Emphasis on lectures or expert panels featuring adult authority figures (NLC, JLO)
Relational leadership group	Ability to manage interpersonal dynamics for the good of the group	Espoused focus on "quiet leaders" at NLC; pedagogical focus on dynamics at IJL
Service leadership	Commitment to engaging in activities dedicated to helping underserved or needy populations	Trip to soup kitchen with JLO
"Great individual" leadership	Recognition of one or two individuals as "the best"	Evaluation and selection process at NLC
Intellectual leadership	Ability to reason clearly and persuasively in a manner that influences others	"Family time" at NLC; group discussions at all programs
Moral and spiritual leadership	Commitment to the cause of promoting social justice	Street Torah at JLO; segregation exercise at IJL

are closely aligned with theories that have already been extensively studied. For example, the notion of intellectual leadership is closely related to work done by Howard Gardner.[23] Service leadership has been explored extensively.[24] The notion of charismatic leadership has received considerable attention by scholars of adult leadership.[25] A complete overview of the connections between the literature on adult leadership and the practice of youth leadership is beyond the scope of this research but would surely be of value to a field seeking greater understanding of how to promote positive development effectively.

Question 2: What pedagogical techniques are employed by programs to teach the model of leadership they espouse?

Once again, this research is based on a recognition that we know very little about effective positive development practices for youth. While the first question focused on theory, this question was designed to spotlight the actual practices used to teach youth leadership.

A complete list of pedagogies encountered in this research is presented in Table 4.2. This list represents my effort to codify and, I hope, clarify the practices I encountered over the course of my research. It is my hope that the list of pedagogical tools presented here may provide helpful new ideas to educators in the field who may be unfamiliar with some of the activities described here. Perhaps this too may promote more effective educational practice in the field. However, the list also raises some important questions. For the field to advance in its understanding of effective youth development practices, we must begin to move from a simple list of practices to an informed understanding of what constitutes best practices.

Once again, a first step should involve reviewing the wealth of relevant literature. Considerable work has been done, for instance, regarding the effects of involvement in community service projects. Research suggests that participation in service projects has a "salutary effect" on levels of political involvement, religious engagement, and substance use,[26] and that it allows youth to develop identities and relationships oriented toward socially responsible participation in adult life.[27] A complete review of the literature relevant to the wide variety of pedagogies presented in Table 4.2 is beyond the scope of this research. However, as the field continues to explore best practices in positive youth development, an in-depth analysis of the research related to these techniques would be a helpful contribution to both the theory and practice of youth leadership education.

Finally, this research raises many questions for further research. For example, what impact do these fairly brief pull-out programs have on participants? How important are preprogram activities and follow-up activities? How can technology such as the Internet be most effectively integrated into youth leadership programming?

Table 4.2. Pedagogies encountered in this research

Pedagogical tool	Definition	Example
Lecture	Frontal presentation by an authority to an audience	Keynote address at JLO
Expert panel	Presentation by two or more authority figures to an audience	Mock trial at NLC; AIDS panel at JLO
Evaluation and selection	Formal process of selecting "best" leader	Selection of NLC candidates to continue to world conference
Reflective practice	Time set aside to reflect on feelings triggered by activities of program	Processing of segregation activity at IJL, personal priority list at JLO
Case-in-point learning	Activity in which the real-time group process is the pedagogical focus	Segregation activity at IJL
Large-group discussion	Exploration of issue in a large-group format	Processing of segregation activity at IJL
Small-group discussion	Portion of larger group breaks off for more intimate exploration of an issue	Reflection sessions at JLO
Community service activity	Engaging in actual service project	Work in soup kitchen at JLO

Field trip	Leaving the primary educational facility to visit outside location	Trip to Capitol Hill at JLO
Cheering	Planned communal singing, chants	"Buttercup" at NLC
Material reward	Small token granted to reward desired behaviors	Stickers at NLC
Problem-solving activity	One-time, highly goal-oriented, team-based experience	Egg drop challenge at NLC
Committee activity	Ongoing team-based effort to plan or execute another event	Planning of visit to member of Congress at JLO
Religious text study	Group exploration of sacred texts	Bible quote debates at JLO
Out-of-context programming	Bringing together diverse youth away from their home communities	NLC, JLO, IJL models
Preprogram activities	Preparing participants for program with activities that occur before out-of-context programming	JLO curriculum at Jewish day schools, supplementary schools
Follow-up activities	Continuation of engagement with ideas presented at out-of-context program after participants return home	Planning community service activity following JLO; involvement of alumni at NLC

Ultimately, this exploratory research represents just the beginning of a process of bringing attention, clarity, and academic rigor to the study of youth leadership education.

Notes

1. Csikszentmihalyi, M. (1990). *Flow: The psychology of optimal experience.* New York: Harper Perennial. Larson, R. W. (2000). Toward a psychology of positive youth development. *American Psychologist, 55*(1), 170–183. Seligman, M., & Csikszentmihalyi, M. (2000). Positive psychology. *American Psychologist 55*(1), 5–14.

2. Cornerstone Consulting Group. (2000). *Common principles of successful youth development programs: A guide to key characteristics.* Houston: Cornerstone Consulting Group.

3. Benard, B. (1991). *Fostering resiliency in kids: Protective factors in the family, school, and community.* Portland, OR: Western Regional Center for Drug-Free Schools and Communities. Deci, E. L. (1995). *Why we do what we do: The dynamics of personal autonomy.* New York: Putnam. Jessor, R., Van Den Bos, J., et al. (1995). Protective factors in adolescent problem behavior: Moderator effects and developmental change. *Journal of Developmental Psychology, 31*(6), 923–933. Brandtstadter, J. (1998). Action perspectives on human development. In R. M. Lerner (Ed.), *Theoretical models of human development.* New York: Wiley. Larson. (2000).

4. Larson. (2000). p. 170.

5. Stogdill, R. M. (1974). *Handbook of leadership.* New York: Free Press. Bass, B. M. (1981). *Stogdill's handbook of leadership* (revised ed). New York: Free Press. Rost, J. (1991). *Leadership for the twenty-first century.* Wesport, CT: Praeger. Heifetz, R. (1994). *Leadership without easy answers.* Cambridge, MA: Belknap Press of Harvard University Press.

6. Rost. (1991). pp. 6–7.

7. van Linden, J., & Fertman, C. (1998). *Youth leadership: A guide to understanding leadership development in adolescents.* San Francisco: Jossey-Bass, p. 6.

8. Ibid.

9. Burrington, Fortier, et al. (1995). *Youth leadership in action: A guide to cooperative games and group activities written by and for youth leaders.* Dubuque, IA: Kendall/Hunt.

10. McLuen, D. W., & Wysong, C. (2000). *The student leadership training manual for youth workers.* Grand Rapids, MI: Zondervan.

11. MacGregor, M. (2000). *Leadership 101: Developing leadership skills for resilient youth.* Denver: Youthleadership.com.

12. Wyman, L., Brookes, H., et al. (1999). Leadership giftedness: models revisited. *Gifted Child Quarterly, 43*(1), 12–24.

13. Heifetz. (1994). p. 18.

14. Parks, S. (1997). *The art of learning leadership.* Cambridge, MA: Lilly Endowment.

15. Merriam, S. B. (1998). *Qualitative research and case study applications in education.* San Francisco: Jossey-Bass. Charmaz, K. (2000). Grounded theory. In N. K. Denzin & Y. S. Lincoln (Eds.), *Handbook of qualitative research.* Thousand Oaks, CA: Sage.

16. Yin, R. K. (1994). *Case study research: Design and methods* (2nd Ed.). Thousand Oaks, CA: Sage.

17. Ibid. Merriam, S. B. (1998).

18. As my research involved exploring diverse pedagogies, as opposed to diverse adolescent populations, I defined no specific criteria for participant gender, race, religion, or socioeconomic status factors that had to be included in this sample.

19. Miles, M. B., & Huberman, A. M. (1994). *Qualitative data analysis.* Thousand Oaks, CA: Sage. Yin, R. K. (1994). *Case study research: Design and methods* (2nd Ed.). Thousand Oaks, CA: Sage.

20. I was able to gather feedback from the directors of all programs except for the NLC.

21. Four graduate students from the Harvard Graduate School of Education analyzed a sample of my data.

22. Wyman, L., Brookes, H., et al. (1999).

23. Gardner, H. (1995). *Leading minds: An anatomy of leadership.* New York: Basic Books.

24. Youniss, J., Yates, M., et al. (1997). Social integration: Community service and marijuana use in high school seniors. *Journal of Adolescent Research, 12*(2), 245–262. Youniss, J., McLellan, J., et al. (1999). The role of community service in identity development: Normative, unconventional, and deviant orientations. *Journal of Adolescent Research, 14*(2), 248–261.

25. Willner, A. R. (1984). *The spellbinders: Charismatic political leadership.* New Haven, CT: Yale University Press. Conger, J. A. (1989). *The charismatic leader: Behind the mystique of exceptional leadership.* San Francisco: Jossey-Bass.

26. Youniss, J., McLellan, J., et al. (1999).

27. Youniss, J., Yates, M., et al. (1997). Larson, R. W. (2000).

MAX KLAU *is senior researcher for leadership and evaluation at City Year in Boston. He received his Ed.D. in June 2005 from the Harvard Graduate School of Education, where he focused his studies on youth leadership.*

The Innovation Center for Community and Youth Development is a Washington, D.C.-based organization engaged in programming, research, and policy development related to youth civic engagement. Its mission is to unleash the potential of youth, adults, organizations, and communities to engage together in creating a just and equitable society.

5

Leading, learning, and unleashing potential: Youth leadership and civic engagement

Wendy Wheeler with Carolyn Edlebeck

LEADERSHIP IS ABOUT learning, listening, dreaming, and working together to unleash the potential of people's time, talent, and treasure for the common good. Too often, young people are excluded from community leadership roles, or relegated to age-segregated opportunities such as service learning and youth commissions. Young people are not only key stakeholders of a community, but they also represent a huge and often untapped reservoir of human energy, talent, and vision. Youth civic engagement works to unleash this potential to create individual, local, and society-level change.

Plenty of young people will not ever be found in traditional youth development organizations. These young people tend to be older, more challenged, and less likely to participate in group activities. As a result, many organizations write them off as alienated and impossible to reach.

Through the Innovation Center's work with organizations and communities across the United States and the world, we have found that these young people can find a place for themselves in organizations focused on civic activism. They are ready and willing to get involved when it means they can act on their own values and bring about changes that will affect their daily lives and the lives of people about whom they care.

Some civic activism organizations have become successful youth leadership programs. Working outside the realm of the traditional youth development world, they have invented creative ways of engaging young people, challenging them, and spurring them to achieve more than either the organization or the young person might have accomplished alone. Youth leadership programs that achieve great outcomes with youth employ the following four strategies for success:

- Build young people's connections to their own identity, culture, and community.
- Recognize that young people are assets to and experts about their own communities.
- Engage young people as community leaders on issues that matter to them.
- Create developmental opportunities that are sustained and supported over time.

A fifth strategy, to bring young people and adults together to work as equal partners, is pushing the understanding of not only youth leadership but also the fundamental concepts of community leadership development.

Build young people's connections to their own identity, culture, and community. In communities across the country and around the world, organizations are working with young people to help them understand who they are, where they came from, and what their heritage offers them. Armed with this understanding, young people can appreciate their own identity, understand how historic injustices affect them, and use this knowledge to make positive changes.

These programs support critical thinking skills and instill in youth the values and attitudes that help them recognize and take action against injustice. Often these programs also create a positive, safe space for marginalized young people to explore their identity as a part of fostering positive development.

Recognize that young people are experts on their communities. Ask a young person about his or her community and you will hear perceptive insights and clear ideas about ways to improve it. Ask a few more questions and you may find deep passion for equity and the desire to make the world better.

Too frequently, adult-directed community service is the only pathway of civic engagement open to young people. While service is important, such programs often offer young people only passive roles in which outcomes are counted in terms of hours served, not in results achieved. When adults write off youth as inexperienced and view them simply as passive service providers, they miss out on some of the richest resources in their community. Just as important, young people miss out on a chance to make a real difference, build their own skills, and gain the confidence that comes when others value their work.

Engage young people as community leaders on issues that matter to them. Through civic engagement, young people can channel their frustration with injustice and devote energy to leadership for positive change. Driven by a desire to create change, they are ready and willing to take on leadership roles—and to develop the skills to do the job well. Organizations that capitalize on this interest can help young people develop new competence, confidence, and long-term goals through the experience, while at the same time gaining from the passion, creativity, and strengths that young people bring to their work.

Create developmental opportunities that are sustained and supported over time. Often youth leadership is perceived as a one-time opportunity for a young person to contribute. For many educators, the toughest part of youth leadership development is creating structures for ongoing growth and pathways for the application of the learning in action. In order for youth to be successful, they need continued support in the form of consistent, structured activities that deepen knowledge, commitment, and opportunity for action.

Bring young people and adults together to work as equal partners. Young people's enthusiasm, energy, idealism, and capacity for innovation have served as a catalyst for social change across time and culture. Yet they cannot do it alone. True community leadership is inclusive. It requires crossing the boundaries of age, culture, background, and political beliefs. It demands openness to seeking the new—opportunities, potential, understanding—while building on the old—traditions, experience, history. It is about youth and adults learning and leading together as partners for community change.

Recent advancements in the understanding of leadership development have highlighted the importance of transformational relationships and change. This is an area that is only beginning to be understood in the field of youth leadership development. For those who approach leadership as an opportunity to engage in transformational relationships with others, the potential, results, and rewards of their work are unimaginable and boundless. Youth-adult partnerships are intentional relationships between youth and adults that afford each person equal access and opportunity to learn from the other, use their skills, dream together, and engage in community change and leadership.

In the work of the Innovation Center, youth-adult partnerships are a vehicle for contextualizing learning and youth civic engagement. Place-based experiential learning among youth and adults together allows both parties to build new knowledge, skills, and understanding of themselves and their community, and to engage an intergenerational lens to discover new perspectives and potential for action.

Youth-adult partnerships in collective learning and action promote leadership that is

Effective, responding to diverse community needs and building sustainability

Inspiring, as people realize they need each other and the opportunity to work in cross-generational partnerships; hope, new understandings, and previously unknown dreams and possibilities are all unleashed

Mutually dependent, where the "declaration of interdependence" among individual partners spreads to an understanding of the importance of crossing boundaries and contributing to the common good

Strong relationships between youth and adults create patterns of opportunity for idea sharing, dreaming, and decision making that, when infused into community change initiatives, can lead to powerful results.

Sustaining community change depends on engaging participants from diverse sectors of a community in the process. Too often, isolated pockets of a community—people already connected to one another by virtue of age, ethnicity, class, neighborhood, or religious affiliation—work collectively on behalf of the community to create positive change, only to finish their work with a job done, even a problem solved, but without sustainable community results. This happens in part because the process has not been inclusive from its inception, often because people do not know how. Inclusion requires skills, specific processes, and in many cases a paradigm shift.

Another shift requires embracing mutual learning. The paradigm of mutual learning requires two things: a deep commitment to it and an intentional application of it. The deep commitment includes genuine humility; no one can believe they have all the answers, or that the answers they have will apply to any given situation. It also demands attention to the variety of ways people learn, trusting informal learning as much as, if not more than, formal learning.

The *genuine partnership* paradigm replaces the notion, precious to many, of empowerment. "Usually," says Eric Jolly, president of the Minnesota Science Museum and chair of the Innovation Center's board of directors, "empowerment means I'll get behind you and push you into the fray." Empowerment assumes just one party has something to give the other. Partnership assumes each can learn from the other and already possesses gifts to bring to the process.

Genuine partnership requires humility, mutuality, openness, and the willingness to share ownership for any new idea or understanding. Genuine partnership requires shared commitment and openness to a common vision of a just and equitable world. It requires trust and flexibility. It requires the willingness to try new things and learn from them, to consider them valuable, even if they fail.

Being able to implement these strategies requires a sophisticated approach to organizational development, a willingness to lead with values, and an in-depth understanding of community needs and desires. The results are well worth the effort.

Experiences of a young leader

Carolyn Edlebeck, seventeen, began her work with the Innovation Center in the sixth grade as a member of the Waupaca Healthy Community-Healthy Youth group. Here she relates her experience as a leader creating change within her community and herself.

To me, leadership means being open-minded, respectful, and receptive, eliciting ideas from others while being confident enough to speak your own mind. It means being optimistic and open to the contributions and gifts of everyone, helping them unleash their own potential while not being afraid to unleash your own. As a leader in community-change efforts in Waupaca, I have learned how to speak up and be involved, not as a token young person but as an experienced leader with something valuable to contribute to my community. This has not been an easy journey for me or for others in my community. For a long time, youth were thought of as problems, not as individuals with an important voice to share and gifts to help the community. But through dedication, true partnership, and a commitment to our common vision, we have been able to really make a change in the way young people and adults think about the community, organizations, and themselves in Waupaca, with powerful results.

Before I started with the Healthy Community-Healthy Youth Program six years ago, we had no idea what youth and adults creating positive change would look like. Sharing power felt strange for both young people and adults. It required shifting our perceptions and stereotypes and relearning how to interact with one another and to recognize and appreciate the gifts each of us has, regardless of age. It was not easy, but the results were well worth the effort.

Through my experiences I have been able to learn a lot about leadership and how young people can play a crucial role as equal partners with adults in community change. Everyone, including adults, young people, and organizations, needs to make a conscious effort to reach out and really welcome and appreciate what everyone else brings to the table. In Waupaca we have made presentations to a number of local organizations to raise awareness of our work in the community and ensure that a diverse group participates. We make sure that not just the typical "high-achieving" young people are offered opportunities, but that everyone is invited to share their gifts and strengths with the group. In making presentations we do not just talk about youth engagement and youth-adult partnership; we model it, demonstrating how youth and adults can be equal partners in creating social change. We have been able to recruit so many other leaders of all ages simply by showing them what youth leadership and youth-adult partnership can accomplish.

I have also learned the importance of true respect in engaging young people as leaders. This often means meeting people where they are. In Waupaca, many meetings involving youth and adults are held in a designated room at the school, in the hours before school begins or after school lets out, respecting the requirements that govern a student's day and allowing young people to attend and contribute. It also means providing people with the tools they need to participate fully, not expecting more or less of them because of their age or experience, but helping everyone reach a point where they can contribute. Contrary to what some people believe, young people do want to be involved in the things that matter to them; when given the opportunity to connect, there is so much we can and do accomplish.

In Waupaca our work has led to a lot of change, both in concrete events in the community and in how we look at and address community issues. With young people as equal partners and leaders with adults, we have been able to look critically and creatively at our community's needs and possibilities and together we have created a popular and cost-effective skate park, have encouraged private organizations such as the Lions to engage young people in their work, and perhaps most important, we have created a history and structure for youth and adults to work meaningfully together on committees and commissions that make real decisions about our community. When we started, young people were never consulted and rarely considered in decisions that affected us. Now young people serve on a number of organizational and city council boards as full voting members. We have just begun a three-year process to re-envision what we want for the community. I have been one of the leaders in this work, connecting with the school board, mayor, local priests, business leaders, and others to engage the full diversity of our community, and conducting surveys and leading sessions to help young people and adults celebrate our achievements and assess our reality, and helping us all work together to plan for the future of Waupaca.

New young people are involved in our community every day. Many do not realize they can be leaders and have never been asked to play that role, but when they are challenged to speak out about their community and when their voices are respected, they add amazing ideas, suggestions, and energy to our discussions. Young people have so much to add, and there is so much that a community can achieve when young people are involved, active, and leading the change.

WENDY WHEELER *is founder and president of the Innovation Center for Community and Youth Development.*

CAROLYN EDLEBECK *is a junior at Waupaca High School in Waupaca, Wisconsin, and a lead trainer with the Innovation Center's national training cadre. She is currently considering a degree in international relations.*

"Leadership is not the filling of a pail; it is about the igniting of a fire."—W. B. Yeats

6

Moving from "youth leadership development" to "youth in governance": Learning leadership by doing leadership

Carole A. MacNeil with Jennifer McClean

As an educator, I know that people do not learn by being told the answers. Education is not a process of filling up learners with new information; it is a process of creating conditions that support learners in making discoveries themselves, then putting those discoveries to use. The same holds true for learning leadership. Sure, you can learn about leadership by studying the theories or hearing the stories or writing a reflection paper. But there is a significant difference between learning about leadership and learning leadership. Learning leadership happens experientially, through involvement in opportunities to practice the skills, experiment with approaches, and try on the roles.

What does this mean for youth leadership development? It means we must create opportunities for young people to do more than hear stories of great leadership or participate in skills-building activities. We must work to create those contexts and relationships where young people can engage in the action of leadership, where they can practice and demonstrate leadership in an authentic and meaningful way.

In much of my work I use the language of "youth in governance" rather than "youth leadership development." A youth-in-governance approach pushes me to think beyond programs that help youth develop leadership skills and toward contexts that offer youth opportunities to practice leadership. There are several reasons, both philosophical and practical, that I have made this shift. Philosophically, I believe that focusing on youth as tomorrow's leaders can be a way to prevent young people from having real voice and power today. When I focus too narrowly on the future leadership roles of youth, I might overlook the need to address what current leadership roles are (or are not) available to young people. Further, I believe that our organizations and communities miss out when we simply work to prepare youth for leadership in the future. We need leaders now.

From a purely practical perspective, it is my role as an organizational leader to focus on strategies for achieving our mission as an organization; that work includes thinking about the quality and content of programs and examining the systems and structures in place that support our youth development efforts. Some emerging research suggests that organizations doing civic engagement or activism work with youth do a better job at positive youth development (building skills, knowledge, and competencies) than those with a strict focus on youth development.[1] There are powerful and important differences in outcomes when we engage young people in authentic experiences where they have voice, influence, and decision-making power (or to say it another way, where they are exercising leadership, not simply learning about it). We do not get the same outcomes when we engage youth in "mock" experiences or simulations of decision-making roles.

Thus, a "youth-in-governance" approach speaks to both practical and philosophical concerns. I might be looking for more effective strategies for youth leadership development and realize that leadership practice was a critical component of real learning. Or I might be looking for ways of strengthening my organization and realize that drawing from the insights, experience, energy, and perspectives of young people would help improve organizational learning and decision making. Either way, I seem to wind up at the same place: we need to ensure that young people move into authentic and meaningful leadership roles at the program and organizational levels, where they have or share voice, influence, and decision-making power.

For many years I have focused on addressing organizational supports or barriers for the development and practice of youth leadership (or youth in governance), and on creating policies and practices that include youth in organizational decision making (for example, statewide advisory committees, boards, and search committees). There have been many "lessons learned," through both successes and failures. While there is no magic recipe for success, some strategies for engaging in this work have emerged.[2]

1. Organizations must assess and address the attitudes and beliefs of those who will be involved in the changes. This includes the assumptions held by adults about youth, and vice versa. Do adults believe that the inclusion of youth is simply "good for youth" or do they see it as mutually beneficial?
2. Organizations must clearly articulate the expectations for staff or volunteers in working with youth as decision makers. Is the integration of youth the responsibility of all staff? What is the time commitment expected of staff?
3. Organizations must clarify the roles and responsibilities for youth board or committee members or youth staff. Are they different from adult roles (and if they are different, does the difference facilitate or hinder authentic youth roles)?
4. Organizations must allocate resources to support the integration of youth in an ongoing way. These may include financial resources (for example, transportation or travel costs), human resources (for example, adult partners), or physical resources (for example, office space for youth partners).
5. Training should be made available for both youth and adults to support their work in a youth-adult partnership. Repeatedly youth have told me, "Don't set us up by giving us responsibility

without the skills." They have also shared that the adults needed more skills in learning to work with them (particularly around sharing power).
6. Organizations should develop a plan for monitoring and evaluating the integration of youth. These may include individual performance assessments for both youth and adults (How well did I perform in this group?), evaluations of group process (How well did we work together?), and evaluations of group product or outcome (What did the group accomplish?).

When I reflect on the outcomes I have witnessed from these kinds of organizational changes, I look through two lenses, that of educator and that of organizational leader. Certainly the young people who participate in these organizational leadership roles hone their skills in multiple ways. Youth leaders may increase their group process skills, facilitation skills (the facilitator role is often shared), presentation skills, interview and other job search skills (particularly through serving on a search committee), and decision-making skills. But the positive outcomes extend beyond skills development. There is a shift in the levels of expectations of both youth and adults that I find particularly exciting. During a spontaneous listserv conversation after one meeting, a youth committee member commented, "I am amazed at how cohesive we are, and how much we have been able to accomplish." An adult member added, "It is amazing how much we accomplish as a team." Young people and adults alike begin to see youth as current leaders, not future leaders. They begin to understand that the discussions are richer and the decisions more effective because of the participation of youth. It shifts from something *we* (adults) do for *them* (youth), to something we all do together because it makes sense for all of us, and for the organization. Research indicates that my personal experiences are not unique, that when young people are engaged in authentic leadership and decision-making roles, there are benefits both to adult partners and to the organization.[3]

I am also convinced that the role of my youth partners in revising these decision-making structures has been critical. For example, during the first meeting of a restructured statewide decision-making committee, my youth partner, Jennifer, and I shared responsibility for doing an orientation. Jennifer conducted a mini-training on youth-adult partnerships, creating a dialogue for members to explore the benefits and challenges of working together. That laid a foundation that served the group for the rest of the year together. It helped the committee agree on a set of group commitments that would guide their interactions throughout the year. And it made it safe and acceptable to talk about the challenges of youth and adults leading together and sharing power.

Conclusion

These days I find myself thinking more about systems change and social justice than about youth leadership development *per se*. Whereas I used to ask, How can I be more effective at supporting young people in discovering and developing their own unique leadership strengths? now I find myself asking, What can I do, in partnership with youth and other adult allies, to create system change to address the marginalization of youth? How can I help create openings so that young people have their rightful voice and role in the decisions that affect their lives? That does not mean that programs to support youth leadership development are not important, or that we do not need committed educators to think about the quality, content, and methods of those programs. Rather, the question for me is about what comes next: How can I make sure that the young person, learning about leadership, learning the skills of leadership, will find opportunities to practice that leadership? How can I make sure that opportunities are available for that young person to engage in the work of leadership, benefiting not only herself or himself, but also the group and organization in which she or he is engaged? If we are to be most effective at supporting the leadership development of youth, we will have to identify or create more authentic opportunities for those youth to practice leadership. That will mean addressing the barriers that prevent youth from having authentic leadership roles in our programs, organizations, and communities (including our own assumptions about "appropriate" roles for young people). But the potential benefits are great: to the youth, to the adults who work with them, and to the organizations and communities that benefit from the emerging leadership of young people.

A reflection on leadership development

Jennifer McClean worked with Carole MacNeil on a statewide decision-making committee. Here she relates her experiences as a youth in governance.

My experience with the 4-H Youth Development Program (4-HYDP) began when I was a seven-year-old living on a small noncommercial farm, following in the footsteps of my older sisters. I joined many projects in my local club, including foods and nutrition, arts and crafts, and dairy goats. Looking back, I know that I immediately began developing leadership skills. But at the time I just thought I was having fun cooking, making crafts, and playing with goats.

As I became older and more involved in the 4-H program, I took on leadership roles in the more traditional sense of that word. I became a junior and teen leader in my projects, chair of club or county events and projects, and a county All Star. (4-H All Stars is an honor and service organization. Their purpose is to contribute to positive youth development through service to the 4-H program of which they are a part.) All of these opportunities helped me hone my leadership skills, but what did that mean? Back then I thought leadership was just a term used to loosely describe what I was doing and learning in the 4-H program. To me, leadership meant taking on greater responsibility, taking action, that my ideas mattered, and that I was given more respect and trust by my peers and adults.

The pieces of the leadership development puzzle started to come together as I became more involved at the state and national levels of the 4-H program. I was a member of the California National

Conference Delegation and was also the California representative to the National 4-H Youth Directions Council (N4-HYDC). These positions gave me opportunities to meet youth leaders from throughout the country and to gain a sense of empowerment. With N4-HYDC, I learned the key components that make up a leader. Emphasis was placed on youth-adult partnerships, which I now believe to be central to the development of youth leadership. I learned that I had actually been a leader all along without ever truly understanding the importance of my work and development. It became clear that I, and other youth, were not leaders of tomorrow but actually leaders of today.

With this new vision of leadership as an immediate rather than future state, I began giving youth-adult partnership trainings with Carole MacNeil, director of California 4-HYDP. Carole and I engaged in a working partnership, not simply a mentorship. Through my work with Carole and our many conversations, I began to understand that one cannot be a leader in isolation. Rather, a leader is a tool, a facilitator, and an active contributor to the team. Within a team there is not one leader but rather a group of leaders; all team members exercise different levels of leadership as they bring their unique skills, perspectives, and personal traits to the tasks at hand.

I started my involvement in 4-H believing that in order to be a leader one had to be the person in charge, directing the actions of others. I now understand that one can be a leader in many more subtle ways. My 4-H experiences and development helped me gain this new perception of leadership. 4-H gave me the opportunity to slowly and steadily experience greater and greater leadership opportunities. Recently I have served as a full member of statewide decision-making bodies, including the Program Advisory Committee, Incentives and Recognition Committee, the Foundation Board of Directors, and the Marketing Task Force. Each of these bodies has an almost equal membership of youth and adults. It was clear from the beginning that these committees sought working youth-adult partnerships where youth and adults have equal decision-making roles. For youth to develop a sense of true empowerment, and a personal definition of leadership, opportunities such as these must be provided where youth can act as equal decision-making partners with both youth peers and adults.

Notes

1. Gambone, M., Yu, H., Lewis-Charp, H., Sipe, C., & Lacoe, J. (2004). *A comparative analysis of community youth development strategies.* Circle Working Paper, University of Maryland.
2. These strategies have become clearer through both practical experience ("trial and error") and through a year-long study of another youth organization attempting to do this work. See MacNeil, C. (2000). Youth-adult collaborative leadership: Strategies for fostering ability and authority. Ann Arbor, MI: UMI Dissertation Services.
3. Checkoway, B., & Richards-Schuster, K. (2001). Young people as agents of community change: New lessons from the field. *Pregnancy Prevention for Youth, 4*(2). Olson, J., Goddard, H., Solheim, C., & Sandt, L. (2004). Making a case for engaging adolescents in program decision making. *Journal of Extension, 42*(6). Zeldin, S. (2004). Youth as agents of adult and community development: Mapping the processes and outcomes of youth engaged in organizational governance. *Applied Developmental Science, 8*, 75–90.

CAROLE A. MACNEIL *is statewide director of the University of California's 4-H Youth Development Program, and national director of the 4-H Youth in Governance Initiative.*

JENNIFER MCCLEAN *will graduate from the University of California Berkeley's Haas School of Business in May 2006, after which she will join Deloitte & Touche in San Francisco. She served on the statewide 4-H Program Advisory Committee in 2002–03.*

The National Conference for Community and Justice is a national organization whose mission is fighting bias, bigotry, and racism in the United States. Camp Anytown, a four-day residential education program for high school students, is one of the organization's primary programs devoted to youth leadership.

7

Anytown: NCCJ's youth leadership experience in social justice

Julia Matsudaira with Ashley Jefferson

THE NATIONAL CONFERENCE FOR COMMUNITY AND JUSTICE (NCCJ) has been running programs dedicated to developing youth leadership through social justice awareness and advocacy for more than fifty years. Originally founded as the National Conference of Christians and Jews in 1929, the nonprofit organization has adapted its programming to the issues and concerns of the communities in which it exists, all while remaining focused on the core mission of NCCJ: to fight bias, bigotry, and hatred in America.

Anytown is the flagship of NCCJ's youth programs. A residential retreat for high school students that typically spans one week, Anytown gives participants an experiential education in leadership grounded in social justice issues. High school students from diverse geographic, socioeconomic, cultural, racial, and religious backgrounds are nominated to attend Anytown by teachers or adult advocates from their schools, places of worship, and other community institutions. Each program participant is considered a representative of the community and background from which he or she comes, so Anytown calls its student participants "delegates." Through interactive exercises, workshops, small- and large-group discussions, and team-building activities, delegates from a broad community learn how to explore differences and discover common understanding based on respect and open communication.

Anytown has been an integral part of NCCJ's focus on youth leadership training through its mission since the 1950s. First introduced through NCCJ's Southern California region, Anytown was then incubated, fine-tuned, and promoted through the Arizona region for several decades. During the 1970s and 1980s, Anytown expansion gained momentum in NCCJ regions across the country.[1] In the summer of 2004, the Anytown model was executed under various names—Brotherhood/Sisterhood Camp, Anytown Youth Leadership Institute, Camp Anytown, and others—in thirty-seven NCCJ regions across the country. To commemorate the fiftieth anniversary of Anytown's national expansion, program staff from NCCJ regions around the country are currently working to share core curricula and materials and firsthand experiences in order "to strengthen and enhance [NCCJ's] signature program."[2]

In the Anytown program manual distributed by NCCJ's national headquarters in 1992, the core assumptions of NCCJ youth leadership programming—and of *Anytown* in particular—are clearly stated: "Commitment to NCCJ youth work is based on a general belief that young people are the nation's future leaders and that the fate of multicultural relations rests in their minds and hearts." Furthermore, the process of social change depends on the individual leadership of these young people turned decision makers who possess an awareness of diverse perspectives and, in turn, "make fair judgments in improving the quality of life for the entire nation regardless of race, ethnicity, gender, faith, or religion."[3]

NCCJ's mission and vision rest on this assumption that our communities will not transform without the action of bold and informed leaders. Based on this set of assumptions, NCCJ has designed programs that provide leaders—both emerging and established—with opportunities to increase the awareness and skills required to serve as advocates and to take action to create just and inclusive communities. As a practitioner of NCCJ's youth leadership curriculum for more than eight years, I have developed the understanding that leadership is not an inherent ability that is bestowed unto some and not others; leadership is a skill that can be developed, honed, and sharpened over time.

At Anytown, young people are taught not only that they are our leaders of tomorrow, but also that they are *already* leaders among their friends, families, classmates, and peers. The influence that young people—teens especially—have among their friends and community is undeniable. Peer pressure and the power that teens have in shaping consumer trends and popular culture are real phenomena. While their assets and contributions to our society are often minimized, teens possess a great deal of influence, especially when it comes to shaping the opinions and behaviors of their peers.

Realizing the power they possess is a critical moment for teens. At Anytown, the focus is first on facilitating that realization, and second on examining how each individual controls his or her power to influence the community. Anytown staff and advisors stress to the delegates that a choice must be made: use the power to influence those around you in positive ways or in negative ways. Anytown clarifies that "not choosing" is in fact a choice; not choosing, whether because of apathy, inaction, or a denial of having power in the first place, in fact promotes the likelihood that those choosing negativity will prevail. The adages "If you are not part of the solution, you are part of the problem" and "Inaction is action" resonate with this point. At Anytown, delegates ask themselves these key questions: Do I want to use my power to influence those around me for the better or for the worse? Will I choose to act or will I stand idly by? Will I be a leader or will I follow?

110   YOUTH LEADERSHIP

High school students are often discounted for being self-centered and unable to conceptualize the impact of their own actions on the world around them. What we often forget, though, is that many of us—not just youth but adults as well—lose sight of the impact of our actions on others on a sadly regular basis. The questions I just mentioned are questions we all face—not just teens. What Anytown realizes and stresses, however, is that teens are at the critical point in their lives when they are beginning to make independent choices and effect changes in their own actions, at least and ideally in their homes, schools, and communities. Anytown provides an atmosphere in which our teenage delegates (not to mention the adult staff facilitators) move through this realization in a systematic, supportive, reflective process.

Before one can understand how to make positive choices and positive change (that is, to be a leader) in regards to any given social issue, it is essential to have a solid understanding of oneself and the nature of one's interpersonal relationships. In its weeklong model, Anytown envisions the exploration of self and relationships to others as incremental stages moving outward, positioning the self at "center." Each day builds on the previous day, focusing on another layer of relationships from self to family, friends, community, and world. For example, day 1 explores self, day 2 explores family in relation to one's self, day 3 explores friends in relation to one's self and family, and so forth.

While delegates are exploring, reflecting on, and discussing their self-identity as it relates to relationships with others, they are also participating in experiential exercises and discussions to raise awareness of social justice issues in our American society: racism, classism, sexism, anti-Semitism and religious intolerance, heterosexism and homophobia, and ableism.

In essence, two major processes of realization and awareness are happening during the Anytown experience. As Figure 7.1 depicts, the Anytown model guides delegates through concurrent processes of self and social reflection. Self-awareness comes through exploration of one's own identity and how the self relates to others and society as a whole. Social awareness of systems in our society comes

Figure 7.1 The Anytown Model

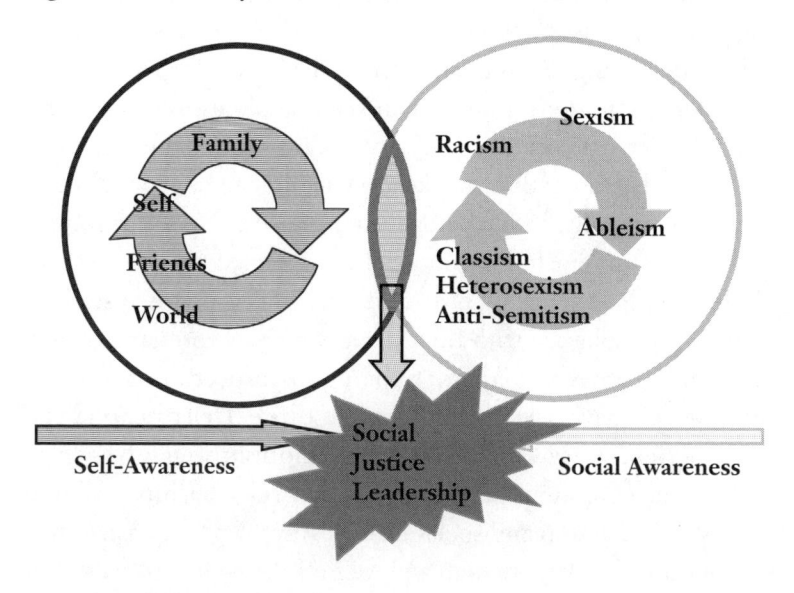

[Diagram: Two overlapping circles. Left circle contains "Self, Family, Friends, World"; right circle contains "Racism, Sexism, Ableism, Classism, Heterosexism, Anti-Semitism". Arrow from left labeled "Self-Awareness" and arrow from right labeled "Social Awareness" converge on a starburst labeled "Social Justice Leadership".]

through examination of how social injustice is experienced and perpetuated by social groups and individuals who capitalize on their power. As self-awareness increases, so does awareness of various social justice issues (sometimes referred to as the "isms").

Eventually, at a critical point in the program, these two processes of awareness intersect: where one's own identity fits within that of society as a whole and how one's own actions interact with the actions of others to promote or prohibit social justice becomes clear. This point—the realization of one's connection to others and to society as a whole, and of one's role as a change agent and advocate for oneself and others—is the conception of social justice leadership for Anytown delegates.

The realization of one's own capacity to be a leader in social justice may happen earlier in the week for some delegates and later in the week for others. Still others may not process and come to this realization until after their week at Anytown is over. It is an implicit expectation or faith, even, of Anytown practitioners that that realization point will occur.

What sets Anytown apart is the way these processes are woven together. Exercises, discussions, and workshops at Anytown are deliberately designed to tap into often deeply held personal experiences and emotions. Rather than keeping discussions on a cerebral or strictly theoretical level, the Anytown model is unique in the way delegates and staff alike are encouraged to express themselves emotionally. Indeed, it is nearly unavoidable for anyone to leave Anytown remaining emotionally disaffected, because we have all dealt with issues of identity and difference. Anytown staff are trained to emphasize with their delegates that expressing oneself emotionally does not equate to being disrespectful or weak, as many people have been taught by adolescence. Delegates' individual experiences are validated. In that emotions weigh heavily in identity development and interpersonal relationships, when it comes to leadership and social justice, Anytown emphasizes that the emotional stakes are high and we must be willing to trust ourselves and each other enough to demolish the emotional barriers that prohibit understanding and communication.

Venues created at Anytown are deliberately designed not only to foster one's own emotional exploration, expression, and transformation, but also to provide the opportunity to witness these processes in others. By witnessing the trials, pain, joy, and triumph of peers—even new friends—together, Anytown lays the groundwork for stronger relationships. Delegates' education in social justice leadership is fueled by the dissemination of information; that education is compounded and cemented by the emotional experience that accompanies the information. Anytown alumni are thereby enabled to develop not just as informed but also as compassionate and empathetic leaders.

It is precisely because Anytown is a program loaded with emotional and deeply personal experiences that it is difficult to communicate as well as to promote the nature of the program's impact on participants. While Anytown is a significant and transformative program for many thousands of teens each year, it does not have the widespread recognition that one might expect for a program conducted by a national organization at this rate and scale. The fact that the Anytown model is executed under different names with various curricula in many of NCCJ's regions further impedes the collection of comprehensive evaluation data tracking the short-term or long-term impact on its participants.

As a six-time Anytown alum who has played every possible role (delegate, counselor, advisor, and codirector), the majority of information I have collected regarding the impact of Anytown on the lives of delegates and their communities is anecdotal and personal. I still carry with me the realization I came to at my first Anytown so many years ago: that I am unique, but I am not alone. For me, Anytown created the physical and mental space away from my everyday life and the obligations of my friends, family, school, and work to really examine my place in it all. I learned that I could confidently overcome my insecurities and build a community based on common purpose and ideals with those around me, simply by reaching out. More than simply introducing me to new information in order to help me logically understand what social justice is or looks like in my community, Anytown forced me to *feel* the consequences of injustice, to relate to the plight of others, and to never forget my role and connection to it all. As has been the case for many other Anytowners I have had the privilege of working and serving with, the Anytown experience awakened me emotionally to the consequences of denying my responsibility as an advocate and a leader.

Reflections from a recent Anytown participant

Ashley Jefferson was a participant at Camp Anytown in the Summer of 2004 and an assistant counselor at Camp Anytown in 2005. Here she tells about her life and what she got out of her participation in Camp Anytown.

I remember my first "really big" decision at my predominantly white school in the town of Reading, Massachusetts. It was our fourth grade Martin Luther King play and I was supposed to play

Martin Jr.'s mother. Kids were already laughing at the fact that my husband had to be white. Now I had to deal with figuring out which doll I should bring to school as a prop. I had many dolls with different skin colors, but I was not sure if I should pick one with light skin or dark skin. People made it worse by asking me in class what color our baby was going to be. "The baby can't be light because Martin Luther King had brown skin, but then again a black person and a white person could never make a dark baby," was all they would say. Ultimately I chose my favorite baby doll, which was coincidentally my skin color. That dilemma was one that I would never forget: it replayed in my head every time I was put in an uncomfortable situation as the only black girl in my classes from fourth grade until senior year. I would hear people switch to speaking slang when they talked to me and make rude and stereotypical comments when they thought I could not hear them. I never said anything because I was uncomfortable. I never said anything because I did not know any better.

I learned a lot from being in Reading, but there were some important things I did not learn there. I knew the importance of individuality, but that was it: I was nothing more than an individual. I never really got it until I went to Anytown. Being placed in circumstances where I had to literally argue for my right to be an individual made all the difference. Why was I born black? Why was I born a female? Sure, I learned all of that in biology class at school. But predicaments similar to the Martin Luther King play always came up and seemed to make me feel bad about who I was and where I came from.

The ability to see the power in all of my differences was given to me at Anytown. The realization that I did have something of value to say was given to me at Anytown. And the knowledge that I could make a difference, regardless of my differences, was given to me at Anytown.

I believe a leader is someone who is an individual and leads with or without followers, regardless of the circumstances. Although a person should admit when he or she is wrong, a person should stick to his or her own instincts most of the time. Going through Anytown was a process that tested our level of understanding of leadership and how sure of ourselves we were. I found myself discussing issues with others that I would not have even thought of beforehand. I can now stand on my own two feet without the approval of others. I will never apologize for my skin color or anything else I was born with. I can make my own decisions without worrying about what others think of me. I no longer fear the thought of standing up for myself when someone talks about how dark I am or how typical it is for me to listen to rap music. That, to me, is being a leader.

Nothing can compare to what I have learned from Anytown. I have started my own organization called the Self-Expression and Activism Project (the SEA Project) where we make connections with each other on issues such as race, gender, and class. Similar to Anytown, we discuss things that people would not normally discuss because they find it uncomfortable. Learning to be an effective communicator is the beginning of becoming an effective leader. For example, we are planning a schoolwide assembly on race and identity. I would not have even thought about anything like that if I had not attended Anytown. For that reason, I attribute every aspect I have gained as a leader to Anytown.

Notes

1. Malcolm, P. (2005, March 1). *Brotherhood/sisterhood camp history*. Available on-line at http://nccjlacamp.org/ourstory/.
2. Schlotfeldt, B. (2005, March 15). Attn Program Staff: Anytown Working Group. Email to All NCCJ Staff ("mailto:jmatsuda@nccj.org").
3. Anytown Manual. (1992). New York: National Conference for Community and Justice. Section I, page 1.

JULIA MATSUDAIRA *was youth program specialist with NCCJ in Boston from September 2003 to December 2004. She codirected Camp Anytown in 2004.*

ASHLEY JEFFERSON *is currently a freshman at UMASS Boston.*

As an independent educator, Eve Nussbaum Soumerai has developed numerous theatrical tributes to inspirational historical figures (Anne Frank, Martin Luther King Jr., and the Dalai Lama, for example). By participating in these productions, young people learn about the lives of these figures and share these stories with large numbers of their peers. Soumerai uses the process of developing and performing these plays as a form of youth leadership education.

8

Arts-Based leadership: Theatrical tributes

Eve Nussbaum Soumerai with Rachel Mazer

THE ARTS PLAY a vital role in the maturation process of our youth. The arts permit freedom of expression in its fullest sense once the evident abilities of individual students merge with those in their inner, yet-to-be-discovered selves. Multimedia read-through plays and tributes to individuals such as Thurgood Marshall, Anne Frank, the Dalai Lama, and Harriet Tubman enable youth to walk through the lives of the honorees while discovering the consequences and importance of individual choice. A group setting and freedom from competition promote the ability to lead. The ethical dimension and awareness of societal needs are fundamental components of tributes and govern the multimedia celebration process.

Origin

On June 30, 1939, I said goodbye to my family, forever, in a crowded waiting room of the Anhalter Bahnhof in Berlin, Germany. Everybody around us was weeping, including my mother. I had but one desire, to leave the scene and go home, but my father, as usual, broke the spell. He smiled, looked straight at me, and said, "You know what?" "What?" I said. "As soon as I get home, I'll write you a long letter," while my sniffling younger brother, Bibi, took the opportunity to ask me for the tenth time to buy him a pair of boxing gloves in England, where I was headed on one of the last Kindertransports to leave Germany. I was thirteen years old and did not yet know how happy I had been, in spite of the Nazis, because of the cocoon my loving family had provided. Two days later I found out. My English guardians, although they wanted to save me from certain death, never had had a child and believed in strict rules and absolutely no frills or "luxuries" such as ice cream or having a friend over more than once a month. I never dared to mention Bibi's desire for boxing gloves.

Two years later, letters and Red Cross messages from my parents had stopped and I stopped caring whether I lived or died. I had become a nuisance. My guardians took me out of school and put me on a train to a residential London County Council nursery school outside of London. I became a helper, and two days after my arrival I again developed an appetite for life. Why? Because I had an intuitive love for children that I inherited from my father, who had spent much of his time with me and my friends. He would tell us stories with funny endings that gave us the ability to listen and laugh while an old phonograph played scratchy records in the corner of our living room. My mother loved Beethoven's Ninth Symphony, which, she told me over and over again he composed after having been deaf for ten years. "Inner music can overcome terrible things and focus on all human beings becoming brothers." She would sing *"Alle Menschen werden Brueder,"* right along with the scratches, made sure I learned some poems by heart, and appreciated the stars, the moon, and the prayers in my black, pocket-sized prayer book.

Searching for answers to what had happened to my family was my major reason for joining the American army of occupation as an Allied civilian employee. I was stationed in Munich near the Foerenwald displaced persons camp. I was eighteen years old and totally unprepared for what I saw and learned on my visits there. But one day I was introduced to a French resistance fighter who had, for a time, worked alongside Albert Camus, editor of the underground paper COMBAT. What I discovered about Camus gave me comfort and energy. Goodness did exist and so did courage. His about-to-be-published book *La Peste* (The Plague) became a blueprint for tribute celebrations, my life's activity. In *La Peste* (a code word for evil, including the Holocaust), everyone is equal and participates—the alcoholic clerk, the physician, the priest, and the anarchist—all help to alleviate suffering and as a result become good, nonjudgmental, dependable friends.

The beginning of multimedia tributes

In 1972, Albert Camus became the very first "guide" honoree at Conard High School, West Hartford, Connecticut. No one had heard of him when I, as newly appointed activities director, suggested we write and produce a tribute honoring him. "Come in and Camus!" became the message in the daily school bulletin. And come in they did in droves, ninety of them, including a school choir that had never before been featured. It was a case of *egalité* and *fraternité*. They read the texts, wrote the script, designed posters, took photographs, and calligraphied Camus' philosophy focusing on justice, honesty, friendship, and love of life on appropriate backgrounds to be used in the form of slides in the production. Albert Camus became the midwife to their creative energies. They argued, sometimes till midnight. They took over. I, the dreamer, became the referee. It was as though the students had been waiting for just such an occasion to find their personal, creative "meaning."

My goal was not to foster youth leadership but rather a way to survive. It became an immersion process for all of us using our individual gifts and tools—hence the multimedia process. Just as in *The*

Plague, everyone was welcome. We all became "brothers" (and sisters!) and contributed to the whole, each in our own way. Some enjoyed being "gofers," others enjoyed cleaning up; some were in the orchestra, all were in the chorus; the emerging student directors were in charge and in consultation with the "gang."

Multimedia tributes thrive

Many honorees followed Albert Camus: Mark Twain, Hans Christian Andersen, Martin Luther King Jr., John Lennon, Thurgood Marshall, Anne Frank, and Harriet Tubman, to name but a few—folks you can rely on not to disappear, because once we have "met" them, they live permanently in our imagination and are always ready to cheer and inspire us like loving parents.

Multimedia tributes are now officially in their thirty-fourth year. There have been changes because of emerging needs. I was appointed Human Rights Literacy director for the National Conference of (then) Christians and Jews. The importance of interdistrict relationships between suburbs and inner cities became a priority and three years of tributes followed. Trumbull High School mentored Bridgeport Elementary School children in a tribute to Langston Hughes. The University of Bridgeport became the performance site and some of their students also volunteered, becoming leaders in the process. A tribute to Langston Hughes was followed by a tribute to the retired mayor of San Juan, Doña Felisa Rincon Gautier, in a bilingual rendition of her life. She graciously received me in her home in San Juan, where I, with her help, wrote the script. She visited Bridgeport and attended the performance.

Student leaders emerge given the appropriate environment—the challenge and the freedom to experiment, to start from scratch, to invent, to become responsible. Is that how we have managed to survive? By appropriate environment, by becoming big brothers and sisters to younger children? A sure win.

What have been the results? The following comments were made by participants in one of the earliest tributes I created and were published in the education journal *The Clearing House* in September 1976.

Steve Amstutz, of the class of 1978, with whom I am still in touch, as I am with many others, commented, "In a world in which so much of life consists of depression and pain, there is a mammoth need to regain confidence in humankind—an ever-increasing prerequisite for survival. . . . Tributes accomplish this by showing man to be basically good; the expression of a much needed outlook."

Sculptor Ana Flores, of the class of 1976, from whom you may hear separately, said, "A mild breeze ruffled our hair on the commodious veranda of the Mark Twain house. This event started my involvement with the art aspect of the Tribute. . . . I began to understand how much students want to know and then share . . . and how they must be given an outlet for their creativity."

Teresa Glennon, of the class of 1977, said, "I was able to use my brain to make my body work. . . . Dancing is a totally different expression than writing or speech. . . . Everything just flowed together the night of the performance. The bond between the cast and the audience was so strong . . . it was more than a show; it was a celebration."

Paul Lundberg, of the class of 1976, said, "I played Dr. Rieux in the tribute to Albert Camus. After one particular taping session we talked far into the night. . . . This tape would cheer me countless times during my first difficult year at college."

A Hartford inner-city fourth grader offered his assessment in 2002 of the tribute to Martin Luther King Jr.: "My feelings about our play are that white people are no better than black people. Our play showed this in the part when the whole school sang 'We Shall Overcome.' Black and white people were holding hands and singing. I think that was the best part. I also think that our audience's favorite part was when Martin and Coretta got married. We got a lot of letters saying that. They also said they liked our singing. One person sang in every song. I think the whole school loved our performance."

I will end with a wish and a feeling, as written by fourth graders Eli and other unsigned students on March 30, 2004: "I wish that the world will be a better place. I would stick up for the inisent. Why do people feel they have to cuase each other pain? (It dose hurt.) I wish I knew."

"If not now, when?"

Rachel Mazer helped create and perform a tribute to Golda Meir in the spring of 2003. Here she discusses her experiences with producing tributes.

I am Rachel Mazer, a freshman at the University of Vermont. Through my personal experiences I have learned that leadership is not a formula. It is a spark that is ignited within an individual and improved through trial and error. Two years ago in Yachad, the Hebrew High School I attended, I was lucky enough to be introduced to teacher and Holocaust survivor Eve Soumerai. I had been told that she was looking for students to research and write a tribute to Golda Meir. A month later, I and other volunteers had completed ten scenes and presented them in an assembly at Yachad. Before this experience with our tribute to Golda Meir, none of us knew anything about Golda and little about Israel. According to Golda's biography, she was proudest of her role as foreign minister in Liberia. Our scene explains how agriculture and water conservation experts from Israel worked alongside Liberians; this was also a scene we presented at the Trinity Boys and Girls club with the kids there. The next tribute I worked on honored Nelson Mandela. We learned in that tribute that Mandela's first white friend was Jewish, and that Helen Suzman, who hired Mandela at the first law firm at which he worked, was also Jewish.

This year I became co-president of UVM Hillel. Our year has been very successful, especially considering the transformation we have undergone in the way we run our organization. Last year we never had more then ten people at a Shabbat dinner. This year we have not had an event that drew fewer than ten people, and attendance at our events has averaged around thirty people. The Chanukah party we had in our Fall 2004 semester was the first time we ever had an event that large. It drew 125 people and was a boost that kept UVM Hillel thriving. This semester we have already decided to start tributes here on campus. Our first tribute will be on 2004 Kenyan Nobel Peace Prize winner Wangari Maathai, who was honored for her "Trees for Democracy" project.

My generation needs to realize that we are the future and that the world will soon be left in our hands. We need to be brave enough to take on that responsibility and reach out to others. This is especially important on college campuses where anti-Semitism is prevalent, and we can use the production of tributes as a solution. When a dance is choreographed that includes the traditional Jewish dance the horah and traditional African dances, and is done with inner-city children, a sense of joy and pride is fostered in both the producers and the participants.

That is why art is so important. It allows us to use our creative energy and unites us. Most important, once the arts are introduced into the tribute, the fun the children are having is evident in their faces, in their delighted eyes. The arts are the vital element that allows us to lead people into learning through this energy.

Tzedek, *Tikkun Olam*, and the constant battle for social justice are Jewish values and goals that make Hillel a legendary organization and give Jews a new avenue to explore their Judaism. As Rabbi Hillel said, "One who is shy cannot learn because he is afraid to ask questions." In accordance with that statement, Rabbi Hillel would love tribute celebrations because they include everybody and do not include competition. Questions, discussions, and exploration of what issues will be important for the future of our world are brought up and are an essential part of each of our rehearsals. Hillel would also agree with our belief, "If not now, when?"

EVE NUSSBAUM SOUMERAI *is an author, teacher, educational consultant, and Holocaust survivor. Currently she focuses on after-school enrichment programs. She is based in West Hartford, Connecticut.*

RACHEL MAZER *is currently a freshman at the University of Vermont.*

Resource guide

Web sites

To learn more about the Youth Leadership Institute, visit www.yli.org. Note their listing of online resources at http://www.yli.org/about/resources.php.

To learn more about the National 4-H Council, visit http://www.fourhcouncil.edu/.

To learn more about the National Conference for Community and Justice, visit www.nccj.org. For information about the Boston Center for Community and Justice, visit www.bostonccj.org.

To learn more about Eve Nussbaum Soumerai's theatrical tributes, visit www.soumeraiconsulting.com/tributes.

Evaluation tools

The PERC (Planning and Evaluation Resource Center) web site is an on-line tutorial and clearinghouse of evaluation and planning tools created in partnership with the Applied Developmental Science Institute at Tufts University. This dynamic site includes evaluation and planning tools, tips, and opportunities to link with others looking to use evaluation to strengthen community youth development programs.

Visit *At the Table* at www.atthetable.org. This interactive, user-driven, Web site allows practitioners of all ages to share resources, strategies, and success stories to support their work in engaging youth in the decision-making process in communities and organizations across the world.

From the Innovation Center

Innovation Center for Community and Youth Development. (2001). *Building community: A tool kit for youth & adults in charting assets and creating change.* Chevy Chase, MD: Author.

Innovation Center for Community and Youth Development. (2002). *Youth leadership for development initiative resource guide.* Chevy Chase, MD: Author.

Innovation Center for Community and Youth Development. (2003). *Creating change: How organizations connect with youth, build communities, and strengthen themselves.* Takoma Park, MD: Author.

Innovation Center for Community and Youth Development. (2004). *Learning and leading: A tool kit for youth development and civic activism.* Takoma Park, MD: Author.

Innovation Center for Community and Youth Development. (2004). *Lessons in leadership: How young people change their communities and themselves.* Takoma Park, MD: Author.

Lewis-Charp, H., Cao Yu, H., Soukamneuth, S., & Lacoe, J. *Extending the reach of youth development through civic engagement: Outcomes of the Youth Leadership for Development Initiative.* Takoma Park, MD: Innovation Center for Community and Youth Development.

Other resources

Armistead, P. J., & Wexler, M. B. (1997). *Community development and youth development: The potential for convergence.* Takoma Park, MD: The Forum for Youth Investment, International Youth Foundation.

Cahill, M. (1997). *Youth development and community development: Promises and challenges of convergence.* Takoma Park, MD: The Forum for Youth Investment, International Youth Foundation.

Camino, L. (2000). Youth-adult partnerships: Entering new territory in community youth work and research. *Applied Developmental Science, 4,* 11–20.

Camino, L. (2005). Pitfalls and promising practices of youth-adult partnerships: An evaluator's reflections. *Journal of Community Psychology, 33,* 75–85.

Camino, L., & Zeldin, S. (2002). From periphery to center: Pathways for youth civic engagement in the day to day life of communities. *Applied Developmental Science, 6,* 213–220.

Carnegie Council on Adolescent Development. (1992). *A matter of time.* New York: Author.

Flanagan, C. A., & Faison, N. (2001). *Youth civic development: Implications of research for social policy and programs* (Social policy report, Vol. 15). Ann Arbor, MI: Society for Research in Child Development.

Gambone, M. A., & Arbreton, A.J.A. (1997). *Safe havens: The contributions of youth organizations to healthy adolescent development.* Philadelphia: Public/Private Ventures.

Gambone, M. A., Klem, A. M., & Connell, J. P. (2002). *Finding out what matters for youth: Testing key links in a community action framework for youth development.* Philadelphia: Youth Development Strategies and Institute for Research and Reform in Education.

Gibson, C. (2001). *From inspiration to participation: A Review of perspectives on youth civic engagement.* New York: Carnegie Corporation of New York.

Ginwright, S., & James, T. (2002). From assets to agents of change: Social Justice, organizing, and youth development. *New Directions for Youth Development, 96,* 27–46.

HoSang, D. (2003). Youth and community organizing today (Occasional paper No. 2). New York, NY: The Funders' Collaborative on Youth Organizing.

Hughes, D. M., & Curnan, S. P. (2000). Community youth development: A framework for action. *CYD Journal, 1*(1).

Kahne, J., Honig, M., & McLaughlin, M. (2002). The civic components of community youth development. In J. Terry (Ed.), *CYD anthology* (pp. 85–88). Sudbury, MA: Institute for Just Communities.

Leadership Excellence Program. (2002). *Leadership Excellence Program curriculum.* Oakland, CA: Author.

McLaughlin, M. W. (2000). *Community counts: How youth organizations matter for youth development.* Washington, DC: Public Education Network.

Pittman, K., & Irby, M. (1996). *Preventing problems or promoting development: Competing priorities or inseparable goals?* Baltimore, MD: International Youth Foundation.

Roach, C., Yu, H. C., & Lewis-Charp, H. (2001). Race, poverty and youth development. *Poverty & Race, 10*(4), 3–6.

Russell, S. T. (2002). Queer in America: Citizenship for sexual minority youth. *Applied Developmental Science, 6*(4), 258–263.

Yates, M., & Youniss, J. (Eds.). (1999). *Roots of civic identity: International perspectives on community service and youth activism.* New York: Cambridge University Press.

Youniss, J., McLellan, J. A., & Yates, M. (March/April 1997). What we know about engendering civic identity. *American Behavioral Scientist, 40*(5), 620–631.

Youth Ministries for Peace and Justice. (2002). *Learning by doing: A manual for youth development and youth organizing.* Bronx, NY: Author.

Youth United for Community Action. (2002). *Political education training manual.* East Palo Alto, CA: Author.

Zeldin, S., Camino, L., & Mook, C. (2005). The adoption of innovation in youth organizations: Creating the conditions for youth-adult partnerships. *Journal of Community Psychology, 33,* 121–135.

Index

Adaptive leadership model, 57, 58, 60–62, 69–70, 73–75, 77–78, 79
Agran, M., 25
AIDS, 74
Alabama, Montgomery, 61
Amstutz, S., 121
Andersen, H. C., 120
Anytown Youth Leadership Institute, 108
Applied Developmental Science Institute, Tufts University, 125
Arbreton, A.J.A., 127
Armistead, P. J., 126
Astin, H., 35, 41
ATOD (alcohol, tobacco, and other drugs), 20
Aung, K., 25

Bandura, A., 49
Bass, B., 41
Bass, B. M., 86
Beethoven's Ninth Symphony, 118
Benard, B., 86
Benson, P., 42
Bliss, S., 4, 9, 13, 25
Bolman, L., 28, 41
Boston, 71, 125
Boyd, S., 1, 6
Boyte, H. C., 56
Brandtstadter, J., 86
Brendtro, L., 56
Brokenleg, M., 56
Brookes, H., 86
Brotherhood/Sisterhood Camp, 108
Burrington, B., 86

Cahill, M., 126
California, 14, 105, 108
Calvert, M., 42
Camino, L., 38, 41, 42, 126, 127
Camp Anytown, 11–12, 107–115

Camus, A., 119–120, 121
Cao Yu, H., 25, 126
Capitol Hill, 73
Carlson, L., 36, 43
Carnegie Council on Adolescent Development, 126
Carnegie Foundation, 60, 69
Charmaz, K., 87
Checkoway, B., 42, 106
Chrislip, D., 36, 43
Clifton, R., 42
Conger, J. A., 87
Connecticut, West Hartford, 119
Connell, J. P., 127
Cooney, E., 6
Cornerstone Consulting Group, 57–58, 86
Csikszentmihalyi, M., 86
Curnan, S. P., 127

Dahms, A., 42
Dalai Lama, 117
Dallas, 71
Deal, T., 28, 41
Deci, E. L., 86
DePree, M., 41
Dewey, J., 49, 56

Edlebeck, C., 11, 89, 94–97
Evaluation and action research (EAR), 19–21

Faison, N., 127
Fertman, C., 59, 86
Flanagan, C. A., 127
Flores, A., 121
Fortier, S., 86
4-H Youth Development Program (4-HYDP), 11, 104–106, 125
Frank, A., 12, 117, 120

129

Gambone, M., 106, 127
Gandhi, M., 61
Gardner, H., 82, 87
Gardner, J., 30, 41
Gautier, D.F.R., 120
Germany, 118
Gibson, C., 127
Ginwright, S., 127
GIRL Project, 20, 21
Girl Scouts, 4, 16
Giroux, H., 32, 42
Glennon, T., 121
Goddard, H., 42, 106
"Great man" theories, 27–28

Hechinger, F., 41
Heifetz, R., 2, 60–64, 86
Helgesen, S., 41
Hesselbein, F., 41
Higher Education Research Institute, 41
Hillel, 123–124
Honig, M., 127
Hope, A., 41
HoSang, D., 127
Huberman, A. M., 87
Hughes, C., 25
Hughes, D. M., 127
Hughes, L., 120

Independent Sector, 41
Innovation Center for Community and Youth Development, 11, 89–96, 126
Institute for Justice and Leadership (IJL), 75–79, 80–81
International Leadership Association, 1
Irby, M., 41, 127
Israel, 122

James, T., 127
Jefferson, A., 11, 107, 113–115
Jessor, R., 86
Jewish Leadership Organization (JLO), 71–75, 78, 81
Jolly, E., 93

Kahne, J., 127
Kearsley, G., 56

Kindertransports, 118
King, M. L., Jr., 12, 113–114, 117, 120, 121–122
Klau, M., 1, 6, 10, 57, 87
Klem, A. M., 127
Kokopeli, B., 42
Krensky, B., 42
Kress, C., 10, 45, 56
Kretzmann, J., 42

Lacoe, J., 106, 126
Lakes, R., 41
Lakey, B., 42
Lakey, G., 42
Langman, J., 41
Larson, C., 36, 43
Larson, R. W., 58, 86
Leadership Excellence Program, 127
Leland, C., 35, 41
Lennon, J., 120
Lewis-Charp, H., 25, 106, 126, 127
Libby, M., 4, 9, 13, 25
Liberia, 122
London, 118
Lowery, R., 56
Luckow, L., 1, 6
Lundberg, P., 121

Maathai, W., 123
MacGregor, M., 86
MacNeil, C., 11, 27, 41, 42, 43, 99, 104, 105, 106
Malcolm, P., 115
Mandela, N., 12, 122
Marin County Board of Supervisors, 15, 20, 21
Marin County (California) Youth Commission, 15, 20, 21
Marshall, T., 117, 120
Maslow, A., 56
Massachusetts, Reading, 113, 114
Matsudaira, J., 11, 107, 115
Mazer, R, 12, 117, 122–124
McClean, J., 11, 99, 104–106
McKnight, J., 42
McLaughlin, M., 25, 41, 127
McLellan, J., 87, 127
McLuen, D. W., 86
Medoff, P., 42
Meir, G., 122

INDEX

Melendez, S., 41
Merriam, S. B., 87
Miles, M. B., 87
Minnesota Science Museum, 93
Mohamed, I., 24
Mook, C., 127
Munich, 119

Napier, R., 42
National Conference of Christians and Jews, 107, 120
National Conference for Community and Justice (NCCJ), 11–12, 107–115, 125
National 4-H Youth Directions Council (N4-HYDC), 105
National Leadership Conference (NLC), 64–71, 73, 80
National Youth Leadership Council, 17
Nazis, 118
Nemerowicz, G., 41
New England, 65
New Haven, 71
Noam, G., 6

O'Connell, B., 30, 41
Offermann, L., 41
Olson, J., 42, 106

Packard Foundation, David and Lucille, 56
Parks, R., 61
Parks, S., 86
Partnerships, youth-adult, 5, 11, 92–94
Philanthropy Learning Network, 19
Phoenix, 71
Pittman, K., 127
Planning and Evaluation Resource Center (PERC), 125
Power, 21–23
Prevention Youth Councils, 15, 20

Richards-Schuster, K., 42, 106
Roach, C., 25, 127
Robinson, J., 42
Rosen, M., 25
Rosi, E., 41
Rost, J., 36, 59, 86

Rowles, E., 25
Russell, S. T., 127

Sandt, L., 42, 106
San Francisco Bay Area, 15, 19, 20
San Francisco Board of Education, 15
San Juan, 120
Schlotfeldt, B., 115
Sedonaen, M., 4, 9, 13, 25
Self-Expression and Activism Project (SEA), 115
Seligman, M., 86
Servant leader, 17–18
Sipe, C., 106
Sklar, H., 42
Smith, R., 42
Social justice, 4, 11–12, 16–17, 23, 107–115, 123
Solheim, C., 42, 106
Soukamneuth, S., 126
Soumerai, E. N., 12, 117, 122, 124, 125
Spears, L., 25
Stein, Rabbi M., 72
Stogdill, R. M., 86
Stoneman, D., 42
Street Torah, 73, 74
Student Advisory Council (San Francisco), 15, 20
Suzman, H., 122

Takanishi, R., 41
Theatrical tributes, 12, 117–124, 125
Timmel, S., 41
Torp, K., 36, 43
Tubman, H., 117, 120
Twain, M., 120, 121

United States, 14, 16, 34, 90, 107
University of Bridgeport, 120
University of Vermont, 122

Van Bockern, S., 56
Van Den Bos, J., 86
van Linden, J., 59, 86
Vygotsky, L. S., 49, 52, 56

Washington, D.C., 71, 89
Waupaca Healthy Community–Healthy Youth, 94, 95

Webster's Collegiate Dictionary, 45
Wehmeyer, M. L., 25
Wexler, M. B., 126
Wheeler, W., 11, 24, 89, 97
Willner, A. R., 87
Work, J., 41
Wyman, L., 86
Wysong, C.

Yates, M., 87, 127
Yeats, W. B., 99
Yin, R. K., 87
Youniss, J., 87, 127
Youth development, 10, 15, 23, 30, 45–55
Youth-in-governance approach, 99–106
Youth leadership: vs. adult leadership, 9–10, 27–40; arts-based, 12, 117–124; and authority, 5, 10, 31–33, 37–38, 40, 61, 74, 77–78; and civic engagement, 11, 31, 89–96; definition of, 23, 28–29, 30, 37, 45, 59–60, 79–82; and diversity, 34–37; education tools, 61–62; feminist framework for, 35–36; inside vs. outside, 4–5, 9, 13–24; issues in, 51–54; in leadership literature, 29–38, 58–60; models of, 6, 18; pedagogies, 83–85; programs, 10–12, 13–14, 63–86; strategies, 19–21, 90, 101–102; understanding, 54–55
Youth Leadership Institute (YLI), 13–21, 125
Youth Ministries for Peace and Justice, 127
Youth United for Community Action, 127
Yu, H., 106, 127

Zander, A., 42
Zeldin, S., 38, 41, 42, 106, 126, 127

Notes for Contributors

New Directions for Youth Development: Theory, Practice, and Research is a quarterly publication focusing on contemporary issues challenging the field of youth development. A defining focus of the journal is the relationship among theory, research, and practice. In particular, *NDYD* is dedicated to recognizing resilience as well as risk, and healthy development of our youth as well as the difficulties of adolescence. The journal is intended as a forum for provocative discussion that reaches across the worlds of academia, service, philanthropy, and policy.

In the tradition of the New Directions series, each volume of the journal addresses a single, timely topic, although special issues covering a variety of topics are occasionally commissioned. We welcome submissions of both volume topics and individual articles. All articles should specifically address the implications of theory for practice and research directions, and how these arenas can better inform one another. Articles may focus on any aspect of youth development; all theoretical and methodological orientations are welcome.

If you would like to be an *issue editor*, please submit an outline of no more than four pages that includes a brief description of your proposed topic and its significance along with a brief synopsis of individual articles (including tentative authors and a working title for each chapter).

If you would like to be an *author*, please submit first a draft of an abstract of no more than 1,500 words, including a two-sentence synopsis of the article; send this to the editorial assistant.

For all prospective issue editors or authors:

- Please make sure to keep accessibility in mind, by illustrating theoretical ideas with specific examples and explaining technical

terms in nontechnical language. A busy practitioner who may not have an extensive research background should be well served by our work.
- Please keep in mind that references should be limited to twenty-five to thirty. Authors should make use of case examples to illustrate their ideas, rather than citing exhaustive research references. You may want to recommend two or three key articles, books, or Web sites that are influential in the field, to be featured on a resource page. This can be used by readers who want to delve more deeply into a particular topic.
- All reference information should be listed as endnotes, rather than including author names in the body of the article or footnotes at the bottom of the page. The endnotes are in APA style.

Please visit http://www.pearweb.org for more information.

Gil G. Noam
Editor-in-Chief

Back Issue/Subscription Order Form

Copy or detach and send to:
Jossey-Bass, A Wiley Imprint, 989 Market Street, San Francisco, CA 94103-1741

Call or fax toll-free: Phone 888-378-2537 6:30AM – 3PM PST; Fax 888-481-2665

Back issues: Please send me the following issues at $29 each.
(Important: please include series initials and issue number, such as YD100.)

_____

_____

_____

$ _____ Total for single issues

$ _____ Shipping charges:

	Surface	Domestic	Canadian
First item		$5.00	$6.00
Each add'l item		$3.00	$1.50

For next-day and second-day delivery rates, call the number listed above.

Subscriptions: Please __start __renew my subscription to *New Directions for Youth Development* for the year 2____ at the following rate:

U.S.	__Individual $80	__Institutional $180
Canada	__Individual $80	__Institutional $220
All others	__Individual $104	__Institutional $254

For more information about online subscriptions visit www.interscience.wiley.com

$ _____ Total single issues and subscriptions (Add appropriate sales tax for your state for single issue orders. No sales tax for U.S. subscriptions. Canadian residents, add GST for subscriptions and single issues.)

__Payment enclosed (U.S. check or money order only)
__VISA __MC __AmEx #_____ Exp. date _____
Signature _____ Day phone _____
__ Bill me (U.S. institutional orders only. Purchase order required.)

Purchase order # _____
Federal Tax ID13559302   GST 89102 8052

Name _____
Address _____

_____

Phone _____ E-mail _____

For more information about Jossey-Bass, visit our Web site at www.josseybass.com

Other Titles Available

NEW DIRECTIONS FOR YOUTH DEVELOPMENT: THEORY, PRACTICE, AND RESEARCH
Gil G. Noam, Editor-in-Chief

YD108 **Doing the Right Thing: Ethical Development Across Diverse Environments: New Directions for Youth Development**
Dale Borman Fink
This issue recognizes the critical importance of guiding young people toward mature decision making in the arena of ethics and explores ways in which that guidance can take shape. Through surveys, observation, and interviews, the chapter authors have designed activities geared to reshape the way youngsters and others think about right and wrong. Studies of teen-oriented chatroom scripts and other online communities highlight the growing trend of adolescents who seem to dwell more online than in their own neighborhoods. Traditional activities such as sports, out-of-class time, and political and community engagement are also examined as sources of social and emotional development.
ISBN 0-7879-8543-0

YD107 **Community Schools: A Strategy for Integrating Youth Development and School Reform**
Joy Dryfoos, Jane Quinn
Although each community school is different from the others, and each community approaches reform in a variety of ways, the common thread is that "schools cannot do it alone." This volume of *New Directions for Youth Development* summarizes the experiences of the Children's Aid Society and Beacons in New York City and other places; university-assisted models in Philadelphia; school-system-generated community schools in Chicago; communitywide councils in Evansville, Indiana, and Portland, Oregon; and Boston's Full-Service Schools Roundtable. The efforts of the Public Education Network to build public will for collaboration and California's statewide Healthy Start Initiative show how it is possible to expand the concepts over larger areas, and the Coalition for Community Schools provides the rationale for national community school legislation.
ISBN 0-7879-8353-5

YD106 **Putting Youth at the Center of Community Building**
Joel Nitzberg
This issue offers an explanation of community-building principles and how they can be applied to working with youth. The chapter authors provide examples of how community building can be connected to youth development and how youth can be change agents. A challenge underlying this approach is to help communities engage youth in change efforts that are meaningful to them. This may mean expanding youth expression in ways that influence community behavior. It also means looking for ways for youth to develop and use leadership skills to influence change. Contributors show how the community-building field emphasizes the importance of networking and building relationships, enabling all members of a community to potentially be change agents.
ISBN 0-7879-8157-5

YD105 **Participation in Youth Programs: Enrollment, Attendance, and Engagement**
Heather B. Weiss, Priscilla M. D. Little, Suzanne M. Bouffard, Editors
This timely volume proposes that to understand and intervene to improve participation in out-of-school time (OST) programs, issues of access, enrollment, and engagement must be considered, and in the context of program quality. Contributing authors pose a three-part equation where participation = enrollment + attendance + engagement, and examine these three critical components of overall participation in out-of-school time programs. Chapters provide research-based strategies on how to increase participation, and how to define, measure, and study it, drawing from the latest developmental research and evaluation literature.
ISBN 0-7879-8053-6

YD104 **Professional Development for Youth Workers**
Pam Garza, Lynne M. Borden, Kirk A. Astroth
Professional development of caring, capable adults who interact with and on behalf of youth is a key issue for youth organizations and agencies committed to creating environments that nurture young people's growth and transition into adulthood. This issue offers a glimpse of some of the innovated, sustained, and coordinated efforts to advance the preparation and support of youth workers based on the principles of positive youth development. Contributors provide examples demonstrating how to support youth work interaction as well as training networks that take common approaches to professional development and outline some of the significant challenges faced in youth worker professional development and their solutions. From defining competencies for entry-level youth workers to case studies that explore the role of colleges and universities in professionalizing the field, this issue serves as a record of the evolution of the youth development field

and a call for its continued progress in building a comprehensive system that can meet the needs of both youth workers and the young people they come into contact with each day.
ISBN 0-7879-7861-2

YD103 **The Transforming Power of Adult-Youth Relationships**
Gil G. Noam, Nina Fiore
Introducing various perspectives that look at the changes in theories, attitudes, approaches, and practices in adult-youth relationships, this issue stresses a model of growth based on partnership and connection over older theories of autonomy and hierarchy between adults and youth. These ways of viewing young people's contributions as extremely important to societal development have to be increasingly embedded in a perspective that young people grow and thrive in relationships and that social institutions, especially families, schools, and youth-serving organizations, have to change dramatically. Contributors also demonstrate how much common ground exists between older and emerging models of youth development and how much work remains to be done.
ISBN 0-7879-7788-8

YD102 **Negotiation: Interpersonal Approaches to Intergroup Conflict**
Daniel L. Shapiro, Brooke E. Clayton
This issue considers the emotional complexities of intergroup conflict. The chapter authors examine the relational challenges that youth encounter in dealing with conflict and, combining innovative theory with ambitious practical application, identify conflict management strategies. These interventions have affected millions of youth across the continents.
ISBN 0-7879-7649-0

YD101 **After-School Worlds: Creating a New Social Space for Development and Learning**
Gil G. Noam
Showcases a variety of large-scale policy initiatives, effective institutional collaborations, and innovative programming options that produce high-quality environments in which young people are realizing their potential. Contributors underscore the conditions—from fostering interagency partnerships, to structuring organized out-of-school-time activities, to encouraging staff-student relationships—that lay the groundwork for positive youth development after school. At the same time, their examples illuminate the challenges for policymakers, researchers, and educators to redefine the field of afterschool as a whole, including the search for a shared lexicon, the push to preserve the character of afterschool as an intermediary space, and the need to create and further programs that are grounded in reliable research and that demonstrate success.
ISBN 0-7879-7304-1

YD100 **Understanding the Social Worlds of Immigrant Youth**
Carola Suárez-Orozco, Irina L. G. Todorova
This issue seeks to deepen understanding of the major social influences that shape immigrant youths' paths in their transition to the United States. The authors delve into a number of social worlds that can contribute to the positive development of immigrant youth. They also provide insight into sources of information about identity pathway options available to those youth. The chapters offer new data regarding the developmental opportunities that family roles and responsibilities, school contexts, community organizations, religious involvement and beliefs, gendered expectations, and media influences present.
ISBN 0-7879-7267-3

YD99 **Deconstructing the School-to-Prison Pipeline**
Johanna Wald, Daniel J. Losen
This issue describes how school policies can have the effect, if not the intent, of setting youths on the "prison track." It also identifies programs and policies that can help schools maintain safety and order while simultaneously reaching out to those students most in need of structure, education, and guidance. Offering a balanced perspective, this issue begins to point the way toward less punitive, more effective, hopeful directions.
ISBN 0-7879-7227-4

YD98 **Youth Facing Threat and Terror: Supporting Preparedness and Resilience**
Robert D. Macy, Susanna Barry, Gil G. Noam
Intended to help clinicians, youth and community workers, teachers, and parents to support resolution and recovery, this volume examines the effects of threat, stress, and traumatic events, including acts of terror, on children and youth. It addresses not only the individual repercussions of threat but also a collective approach to threat. It also illustrates important ways to prevent traumatic situations from having lifelong, negative impacts. These methods involve providing immediate intervention and fostering safety as soon as a threatening incident has occurred as well as preparing children for future threats in ways that enhance feelings of safety rather than raise anxiety.
ISBN 0-7879-7075-1

YD97 **When, Where, What, and How Youth Learn**
Karen J. Pittman, Nicole Yohalem, Joel Tolman
Acknowledging that young people learn throughout their waking hours, in a range of settings, and through a variety of means, this volume presents practical advancements, theory development, and new research in policies and infrastructures that support expanded definitions of learning. Representing the perspectives of a broad range of scholars and practitioners, chapters explore ways to connect learning experiences that happen inside and outside school buildings and

during and after the school day. The contributors offer a compelling argument that communitywide commitments to learning are necessary if our nation's young people are to become problem free, fully prepared, and fully engaged.
ISBN 0-7879-6848-X

YD96 **Youth Participation: Improving Institutions and Communities**
Benjamin Kirshner, Jennifer L. O'Donoghue, Milbrey McLaughlin
Explores the growing effort in youth organizations, community development, and schools and other public institutions to foster meaningful activities that empower adolescents to participate in decision making that affects their lives and to take action on issues they care about. Pushing against long-held, culturally specific ideas about adolescence as well as institutional barriers to youth involvement, the efforts of these organizations engaged in youth participation programs deserve careful analysis and support. This volume offers an assessment of the field, as well as specific chapters that chronicle efforts to achieve youth participation across a variety of settings and dimensions.
ISBN 0-7879-6339-9

YD95 **Pathways to Positive Development Among Diverse Youth**
Richard M. Lerner, Carl S. Taylor, Alexander von Eye
Positive youth development represents an emerging emphasis in developmental thinking that is focused on the incredible potential of adolescents to maintain healthy trajectories and develop resilience, even in the face of myriad negative influences. This volume discusses the theory, research, policy, and programs that take this strength-based, positive development approach to diverse youth. It examines theoretical ideas about the nature of positive youth development, and about the related concepts of thriving and well-being, as well as current and needed policy strategies, "best practice" in youth-serving programs, and promising community-based efforts to marshal the developmental assets of individuals and communities to enhance thriving among youth.
ISBN 0-7879-6338-0

YD94 **Youth Development and After-School Time: A Tale of Many Cities**
Gil G. Noam, Beth Miller
This issue looks at exciting citywide and cross-city initiatives in after-school time. It presents case studies of youth-related work that combines large-scale policy, developmental thinking, and innovative programming, as well as research and evaluation. Chapters discuss efforts of community-based organizations, museums, universities, schools, and clinics who are joining forces, sharing funding and other resources, and jointly creating a system of after-school care and education.
ISBN 0-7879-6337-2

YD93   **A Critical View of Youth Mentoring**
Jean E. Rhodes
Mentoring has become an almost essential aspect of youth development and is expanding beyond the traditional one-to-one, volunteer, community-based mentoring. This volume provides evidence of the benefits of enduring high-quality mentoring programs, as well as apprenticeships, advisories, and other relationship-based programs that show considerable promise. Authors examine mentoring in the workplace, teacher-student interaction, and the mentoring potential of student advising programs. They also take a critical look at the importance of youth-adult relationships and how a deeper understanding of these relationships can benefit youth mentoring. This issue raises important questions about relationship-based interventions and generates new perspectives on the role of adults in the lives of youth.
ISBN 0-7879-6294-5

YD92   **Zero Tolerance: Can Suspension and Expulsion Keep Schools Safe?**
Russell J. Skiba, Gil G. Noam
Addressing the problem of school violence and disruption requires thoughtful understanding of the complexity of the personal and systemic factors that increase the probability of violence, and designing interventions based on that understanding. This inaugural issue explores the effectiveness of zero tolerance as a tool for promoting school safety and improving student behavior and offers alternative strategies that work.
ISBN 0-7879-1441-X

NEW DIRECTIONS FOR YOUTH DEVELOPMENT IS NOW AVAILABLE ONLINE AT WILEY INTERSCIENCE

What is Wiley InterScience?

Wiley InterScience is the dynamic online content service from John Wiley & Sons delivering the full text of over 300 leading scientific, technical, medical, and professional journals, plus major reference works, the acclaimed *Current Protocols* laboratory manuals, and even the full text of select Wiley print books online.

What are some special features of Wiley InterScience?

Wiley InterScience Alerts is a service that delivers table of contents via e-mail for any journal available on Wiley InterScience as soon as a new issue is published online.

Early View is Wiley's exclusive service presenting individual articles online as soon as they are ready, even before the release of the compiled print issue. These articles are complete, peer-reviewed, and citable.

CrossRef is the innovative multi-publisher reference linking system enabling readers to move seamlessly from a reference in a journal article to the cited publication, typically located on a different server and published by a different publisher.

How can I access Wiley InterScience?

Visit http://www.interscience.wiley.com

Guest Users can browse Wiley InterScience for unrestricted access to journal Tables of Contents and Article Abstracts, or use the powerful search engine.

Registered Users are provided with a *Personal Home Page* to store and manage customized alerts, searches, and links to favorite journals and articles. Additionally, Registered Users can view free Online Sample Issues and preview selected material from major reference works.

Licensed Customers are entitled to access full-text journal articles in PDF, with select journals also offering full-text HTML.

How do I become an Authorized User?

Authorized Users are individuals authorized by a paying Customer to have access to the journals in Wiley InterScience. For example, a university that subscribes to Wiley journals is considered to be the Customer. Faculty, staff, and students authorized by the university to have access to those journals in Wiley InterScience are Authorized Users. Users should contact their Library for information on which Wiley journals they have access to in Wiley InterScience.

ASK YOUR INSTITUTION ABOUT WILEY INTERSCIENCE TODAY!